GET THE  XTRAS!

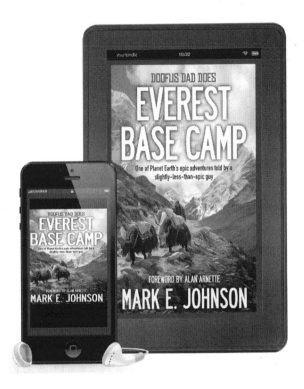

As a huge **THANK YOU** for purchasing my book, I'd like to give you a bunch of cool goodies. Go to *www.doofusdad.com/extras* for free access to videos and photos from the trek as well as gear lists, a training guide, our itinerary, and trek statistics. To learn how you can **download the audiobook for free**, jump to the last page of this book. The audiobook is read by me and contains lots of sound effects from the actual trek. Enjoy!

DOOFUS DAD DOES EVEREST BASE CAMP

ONE OF PLANET EARTH'S EPIC ADVENTURES
TOLD BY A SLIGHTLY-LESS-THAN-EPIC GUY

MARK E. JOHNSON

Cover photo by Bill Shupp. *www.shupp.com*
Cover art by Mark E. Johnson.
ISBN: **978-0-578-21289-0**
Ebook: **978-0-578-21290-6**

For my wife, my children, and anyone willing to exit their comfort zone in the pursuit of something epic.

Standard EBC trekking routes

FOREWORD

I'm fond of saying that if you get a chance to trek to Everest Base Camp or trek in Nepal, take it. It will change your life.

Many people from around the world have made this journey but only a few had the vision and courage to start a trekking business having never even stepped one foot in the country!

Mark and Holly Johnson, from the flatlands of Tennessee, began the journey to Nepal by way of a Nashville Lyft driver named Dawa Jangbu Lama Sherpa. Mark asked Dawa where he was from. Dawa answered "Nepal."

"Hey, I've always wanted to go there!" Mark exclaimed and the rest, as they say, is history. Soon, Hobnail Trekking Company was born.

"Doofus Dad does Everest Base Camp," is a light, easy, and fast read that takes us into the world of trekking in Nepal. If you have never been to the country, seeing it through Mark's virgin eyes is a treat. He brings to life why this country is so special and why it will in fact change your life. If you have already gone or are even a frequent visitor, his vivid writing style brings back the memories of the sights, sounds, and smells.

This book is a must have for the bookshelf of yesterday's, today's and tomorrow's traveler.

Alan Arnette
Mount Everest, K2 summitter, named "one of America's most respected chroniclers of Everest" by *Outside* magazine. Visit Alan's blog here at *www.alanarnette.com*

PREFACE

Doofus: A stupid, incompetent, or foolish person. (Merriman-Webster Dictionary)

I never considered myself a doofus.

In fact, during my younger years, I was widely considered to be cool by many people other than myself.

"Johnson?" people would say. "Oh, he's cool. Definitely."

For some fifteen years, I traveled the country supporting myself as a solo club musician. I had long hair, often played gigs at tropical resorts, stayed tanned, and was quite the Man About Town. I played chick-magnet James Taylor music and wore Caribbean choker beads. I even got tatted, back before everyone had a tattoo.

I was the *anti*-doofus.

Older, clearly *un*-cool men would come to me, asking for advice.

"Please, Rock Star Guy, tell us how not to be doofuses!" they would implore. "How can we be cool again?"

I would shake my head and pat their shoulders with compassion.

"It can't be taught," I would say. "You must be born with it."

Poor fools, I would think to myself as they walked away, dejected. *As if they could ever be as cool as me!*

And then I got married and had children.

Just that alone wasn't enough to throw me into a doofus status. On the contrary, I married a hot, smart woman and for years, was Captain Superhero Daddy who could do no wrong as far as my three kids were concerned.

Then my two older children hit their teen years.

And Something Happened. It was the classic butterfly metamorphosis, in reverse. I devolved from a butterfly back into a worm.

A doofus worm.

Just like that, my coolness became a thing of the past. I didn't recognize the popular singers, didn't know what clothes were in fashion, and couldn't understand the cutting-edge colloquialisms of the young, let alone use them properly.

"I'm out here tryna cook dinner," I'd say to my teenagers, holding a spatula.

"No, Dad," my daughter would reply. "Never say that again."

It wasn't that I had become incompetent in real life. After hanging up my guitar, I worked as a freelance writer and communications professional for twenty years. Many perfectly sane people considered me (somewhat) "smart" and "accomplished" and "not a doofus."

My dramatic fall from grace was mostly in the eyes of my teenaged children, but after a while, you start to believe your own bad press, even from kids. And that is how I took on the role of Doofus Dad without realizing it. I began wearing denim shorts, used phrases like "good grief," and became too well versed in the workings of a barbecue grill. Instead of watching edgy shows like "Nip/Tuck," I went back to "The Andy Griffith Show" (the greatest show ever).

As the years passed, I decided to embrace my Doofus Dad persona rather than fight it. It's so much easier to fly under the radar and out of the paparazzi's glare when so little is expected of you.

That's why the concept of my not only trekking to Mt. Everest Base Camp, but also launching a Nepal trekking company, so shocked the world that its rotation nearly ground to a halt. I'll save the details of how Hobnail Trekking Co. was born for later because it's so crazy, it may distract you from the business at hand.

I've written this book for three reasons: 1) to provide a very honest, helpful, and hopefully entertaining account of the EBC trek for travelers considering this adventure for themselves; 2) to provide hope and the promise of an epic future for all you fellow Doofus Dads and Hot, Smart Moms out there, and; 3) to become stupid rich and famous and have this book made into a blockbuster motion picture.

(Holly has already made it clear that she wants to play herself, but votes for Brad Pitt to play me. I'm not sure how I feel about this.)

My point, if I may continue, is that even plain ol' normal folks like us can embark on epic adventures and complete them in one piece. As a result, our teenagers might even think we're cool again.

But probably not.

～

Mt. Everest: Known in Nepal as Sagarmatha and in Tibet as Chomolungma, Mt. Everest is Earth's highest mountain above sea level. (Wikipedia)

Until recently, my knowledge of Mt. Everest had been no greater than the average second-grader's. We learn that Everest is the world's tallest mountain in what — first grade? Thank you, World Book Encyclopedia.

Tallest mountain? Everest.

Fastest land mammal? Cheetah.

Food that'll most make you gag? Brussel sprouts.

As we become more knowledgeable, we learn that climbing Mt. Everest is at best a risky adventure and at worst practically suicide. The mountain is a literal graveyard of frozen bodies that might still be sitting in the same general spot a hundred years from now. I don't guess that most of those people intended to end up that way. Given the option, they'd probably rather be somewhere else right about now.

So invite the average person who's smarter than a second-grader to venture up Everest with you, and you're likely to be met with suspicion, concern, or some type of phrase that contains a string of keyboard symbols if written out.

"Are you $@*^% crazy??" for example, which makes speaking the sentence impossible unless you replace the symbols with the word you were trying to avoid in the first place.

This was often the response Holly and I received when we first began mentioning to people our impending trip. Sometimes, we would have to physically restrain folks and slap them around until we could make them understand that we were not planning to actually *climb* the mountain, but only hike to the bottom of it.

Big freaking difference and much less dangerous.

Each year, somewhere around 30,000 people do the Everest Base Camp trek. (From here on out, I'll refer to it Everest Base Camp as EBC.) Most hail from other places in the world, usually somewhere closer to Nepal and often from countries that encourage their citizens to "go on holiday" and stuff like that, as opposed to America, where people are encouraged to "work until you die."

To most people from where I grew up, going on holiday meant driving to Myrtle Beach, South Carolina, for one week, eating giant plates of calabash shrimp, riding go-carts, buying t-shirts, and getting properly sunburned.

That actually sounds pretty good, now that I think about it.

Anyway, flying halfway around the planet and hiking for two

weeks into a 17,000-feet lunar landscape is not most people's idea of going on holiday, leastways not in the Southern U.S.

So why do it?

Well, that's a very good question, and I was hoping you'd ask.

First of all, let's not confuse this trek with a vacation. It's not. It is, rather, a life-changing adventure that relatively few people will ever do.

My second reason is the key, though.

Every morning, it's unavoidable that I catch a look at myself in the mirror and the face staring back isn't the "cool" one of thirty years ago; it's the doofus one of the present. This face reminds me that every passing day is one more I can't get back and there's no time like the present to go see and do things. With apologies to everyone who holds with reincarnation, I see life as one body, one trip, one chance.

We had best use it wisely, but with boldness, too.

Trekking to EBC is an opportunity to experience as much *difference* in one compressed block of time as an American possible can.

Different culture.

Different landscape.

Different religions.

Different everything.

At the same time, it provides enough very real physical challenge to be a grand accomplishment minus *too* much risk of losing life and limb.

I can tell that you're tempted to skip ahead, so without any further words to delay you from getting to the beginning of this adventure, let us begin.

AUTHOR'S NOTE

OK, one more quick delay.

The English spelling of Nepali words is a crapshoot. You would think that the government of Nepal would've convened at some point and agreed upon how things would be spelled in English, which is a quite common and oft-used language among locals there.

But no. They haven't done that. Nepal is the Wild West of spelling.

This maddening fact is especially noticeable with the names of things: villages, foods, even people. Depending upon whom you ask, the spelling may be entirely different. You can often find a word spelled one way on a teahouse sign, and spelled differently on another sign — on the same teahouse!

So although I believe the spellings I've used in this book to be the most commonly accepted, you may find them totally different in other books and websites. In fact, you can count on it.

Here we go!

Better to see something once than to hear about it a thousand times.

ASIAN PROVERB

ONE

WINGING IT

For nearly eighteen months, we had been massing our troops, stockpiling supplies, and drilling ad nauseam; now we were the Screaming Eagles, ready to invade Nepal from the sky and attack Mt. Everest.

It was Tuesday, March 27, 2018.

E-Day.

(This was just the day we were scheduled to fly out, but I like to make it sound more dramatic.)

My wife, Holly, and I had launched Hobnail Trekking Co. more than a year earlier as probably the least qualified people on the planet to do such a thing. I'll cover this insane story in my upcoming book, *Doofus Dad Starts a Business*, but the short version is this: I had a chance meeting with then-thirty-one-year-old Dawa Jangbu Lama Sherpa in downtown Nashville, Tennessee, of all places. He was driving for a ride-sharing company and I needed a lift to my mechanic's shop. During the course of the brief trip, I learned to my amazement that Dawa is an Everest Region Sherpa and had been raised in the trekking industry. He had recently moved to the U.S. to be near family and promote his home country.

For more than a decade, since reading Jon Krakauer's novel *Into Thin Air*, Holly and I had become enamored with the idea of trekking to Everest Base Camp. Upon meeting Dawa, opportunity and timing collided in divine kismet.

Within three months, I had resigned from my communications job and was launching a Nepal trekking company, having never *been* to Nepal nor trekked more than about five miles at a time in my life.

And here we were, some eighteen months later, on the cusp of an unthinkable and unlikely adventure.

After saying tearful goodbyes to our kids — I'm pretty sure I heard techno dance music crank up in the house as we rolled out of the driveway — Holly and I drove to her office where we picked up a co-worker, Michael, who would drop us off at Nashville International Airport.

We pulled into a parking space at Departures, unloaded our gear and bags onto the curb, and watched as Michael drove away in our minivan.

Gulp.

My anxiety level was already at Code Red. Aside from the whole traveling across the globe thing, we were also transporting five huge duffel bags filled with new sneakers. Some of our group would distribute these shoes to Nepali schoolchildren as part of a charitable effort organized by the Shuzz Foundation, a Florida non-profit that had piggy-backed onto our trip.

We grabbed a cart, loaded up the shoes, our two Hobnail duffels, and a suitcase, and headed into the terminal.

It was around 2:00 p.m., CST.

It's important to note here that although I love to fly, I hate the airport checking-in process. I've flown out of big airports probably a hundred times in my life, but these flights have never happened often enough for me to gain any knowledge-based comfort or self-confidence.

I always forget how to do it.

Whereas others — sharply dressed, perfect-posture businessmen and woman with slick, rolling carry-on bags — breeze through the check-in and security process with the polished demeanor of martini-sipping Dean Martins, I become a blaring, six-foot-five Jerry Lewis. I'm all flailing knees and elbows. I'm dropping important documents on the floor, answering the gate agent's questions incorrectly, fumbling to return my I.D. to my wallet, and creating a disturbance for the other, normal passengers.

And that's just for an ordinary flight with one suitcase.

So imagine how goofy I became when we approached the counter with enough luggage for the Von Trapp Family Singers, bound for the other side of the planet, some twenty-three hours and three flights away. For these reasons, I babysat the bags while Holly, a.k.a. the Brains of the Operation, handled everything at the check-in counter.

Before we knew it, we were seated on our first flight — Nashville to L.A. — and taxi-ing to the runway. It was 4:00 p.m., CST.

Our reception on this flight was disappointing. Neither the local paparazzi, with their popping flashbulbs, nor the throngs of adoring fans begging for our autographs, ever materialized. Instead, we were treated like plain ol' regular passengers just going somewhere boring, like Los Angeles.

I was wedged into a window seat, knees under my chin, hoping the passenger in front of me would forget about his recline button.

No such luck. Within two minutes of leaving the ground, the guy laid his seat back onto my knees and Holly was sound asleep, snuggled into my shoulder, rendering my right side useless.

I spent the next four hours nibbling on Delta peanuts and mini-pretzels with T-Rex arms.

· · ·

WE LANDED IN THE CITY OF ANGELS AT 7:06 PM, PST. After allowing the circulation to return to my extremities, I followed my well-rested wife off the airplane.

The "adventure" part of the trip kicked in when we walked from our arrival gate down a nondescript and empty hallway and into the LAX Tom Bradley International Terminal. I've been in quite a few airports, but nothing like this. Upon entering the terminal, we encountered a three-story video tower displaying animated whales and fish as the silhouettes of human travelers walked past on a catwalk below.

The main part of the terminal is an upscale shopping mall flanked by additional giant video screens depicting other weird and fascinating graphics. A river of international humanity flowed through the terminal creating an auditory mash up of various languages and dialects, including my own southern Appalachia twang.

After four hours of the best people watching ever, it was time to board the *big* flight, L.A. to Guangzhou, China, aboard an Airbus 380 — the largest commercial jet on Earth.

It was a double-decker plane and we were on the top "floor." I've always wondered how the boarding process on one of these two-story planes works, and now I know. There are *two* boarding ramps, and the second-story people had to climb a flight of stairs to access the top tunnel. Since in many ways, I'm perpetually a twelve-year-old boy, I found this to be simply neato.

We located our seats on the enormous plane. Chinese music floated over the P.A. as we stashed our snacks, ear buds, iPads, and travel pillows within easy reach.

We would be in the air for fifteen hours.

Another tendency I seem to have when flying is to always be in a huge hurry to get situated and buckled in. So within five minutes, I was set up and ready to go.

"Let's do this thing!" I shouted, making the poor lady in front of me jump as if she'd been stung by a bee.

Approximately forty minutes later, the plane began to back away from the gate.

Thirty minutes after that, the plane reached the end of the runway.

After another ten minutes of revving up its engines, the plane finally lumbered into the air.

By this time, Holly had long since re-entered REM sleep, twitching and giggling on occasion. As a wide-awake and uncomfortable human, I had already scrolled through all 235 in-flight movie options on the TV screen mounted into the headrest of the seat in front of me. In fact, I had also *watched* most of the first movie, eaten all of my snacks, and had read "War and Peace."

Twice.

Most alarming of all was the fact that my butt was already getting sore and it was only Minute No. 1 of 900.

I KNEW THIS FLIGHT WAS GOING TO BE INTERESTING, but the weird factor exceeded my expectations, starting with the China Southern flight attendants.

They were the Stepford Wives of flight attendants.

All were roughly the same height, age (early- to mid-20s), and weight. All appeared trim, fit, and by normal Western standards, were attractive. Each was as efficient and professional as the next and spoke just enough broken English to get by. When the safety briefing began, they all bowed at exactly the same time.

I found myself looking for ON/OFF switches and serial numbers imprinted onto their necks as they walked past.

So I had two distinct impressions of the Chinese Stepford Wives flight attendants: first, a Communist country like China can present whatever image of itself to the outside world it chooses without fear of protest or lawsuits by feminist organizations, and the same could *never* happen in America, and second, this flight had the makings of an impressive porn movie — not that I would know anything about that.

ANYway...

Aside from the aforementioned items, the first weirdness occurred after we'd been in the air for less than an hour. We had left L.A. at around midnight and as far as I could tell, were in the same time zone, so an hour after takeoff would've made it around 3:00 a.m. Nashville time.

Dinner is served!

The Stepford Wives proceeded down the aisles of the plane at the same exact pace, handing out piping hot meals to passengers. After shaking Holly awake from her lovely, comfortable dreams, we were somewhat able to discern that the main dish was fish and rice. Exactly what every American needs at 3:00 a.m., right?

Another oddity of air travel for me is that I can always seem to eat anything and everything at any given moment. As soon as I step foot on an airplane, I'm famished. This was no different. I consumed my 3:00 a.m. fish dinner with great enthusiasm, finishing every crumb and demolishing the odd yogurt dessert that came with it.

I considered asking for seconds, but figured that might be frowned upon.

Soon, the trays were collected and the cabin lights were extinguished. As one, comfortable with their well-fitting legs and fish-dinner bellies, hundreds of Chinese passengers and Holly drifted back to sleep within minutes.

There I was.

On the entire vast, second-floor cabin of the Airbus 380 — the largest commercial jet on Earth — the only visible light was emitting from my little entertainment screen.

I felt like a character in the "Left Behind" novels.

Everyone else on the plane — and perhaps, the world — had been raptured into wonderful, comfortable slumber except for me.

I sat there by myself and watched a movie where Winston

Churchill defied the Nazis as Holly snuggled against my left side, now numb.

EVENTUALLY, EVEN I DRIFTED OFF. IT WAS ONE OF THOSE sleeps reserved only for cars or airplanes, where you continue to be aware of the white-noise drone of the engines in your dreams. Mine were all about things like being folded into a box or stuffed under a bed or shoved between elephants or other uncomfortable situations rather than normal dream topics, like making out with Loretta Switt or riding a flying bus with George Costanza.

Obnoxious light blared through my eyelids.

I awoke to the sight of the Stepford Wives and their rolling food wagons coming down the aisles as one.

It was apparently mealtime again.

Holly and I looked at each other with confusion.

What time was it?

Thus began the oddest element of this flight: the time paradox.

We had boarded the plane at midnight and had turned off our phones. After waking from our first "sleep," we had absolutely NO IDEA what time it was. I mean none. Zippo. Our phones didn't work and nothing on the entertainment screens indicated a time, at least not in English. We had left in the dark, we were still in the dark, and would STAY in the dark for the entire fifteen hours. There was no reliable way to know how long we'd been asleep. Could've been two minutes; could've been two hours.

"Is this dinner or breakfast?" I hissed at Holly.

"No idea," came the response.

To make matters worse, there was a choice of meals. We eavesdropped as the attendant tried to explain this in broken English to another non-Chinese passenger, but with little success, so we guessed at which meal to get. It turned out to be some type of omelet thing, so we convinced ourselves it was breakfast time.

"Top o' the morning!" we said to each other cheerfully, bumping our plastic cups together in a mock toast.

But after polishing off our interesting, breakfast-like dish, I peeked out the window and nothing in the blackness suggested that it was anywhere close to morning. I regretted not wearing my analog watch, although the math involved in calculating the current time at this point would've been insane.

Click. Cabin lights off. Within seconds, Holly and her Chinese brethren were raptured into slumber. I moved on to "The King's Speech" starring Colin Firth. For some odd reason, mid-20th century English docudramas seemed appropriate to watch during a fifteen-hour flight on the Chinese Airbus 380 — the largest commercial jet on Earth — while being surrounded by hundreds of snoring people.

The Stepford Wives swished past us in the darkness of the Twilight Zone with demure smiles.

As the interminable night wore on, I watched more movies, played Candy Crush on my otherwise useless phone, and made occasional circuits around the cabin to offset the soreness in my legs. Once, I knocked out fifty air squats in the aisle beside an elderly Chinese man, the sound stirring him half awake. He looked at me long enough to process what I was doing, nodded his approval, and, much to my annoyance, immediately fell back asleep.

SOMEWHERE IN THE MIDDLE OF A JULIA ROBERTS MOVIE, my exhaustion overtook the pain in my lower half and I drifted off again. At some point, I became aware of a slight decrease in engine thrust and the angle of the plane tipping downward. I opened my eyes.

It was still dark outside, of course. The flight tracker app on my screen said thirty minutes to destination. We had nearly completed nearly fifteen hours of air travel over the Pacific Ocean, across the entire island of Japan, and into the interior of China and I never saw a *single thing* outside the window.

The cabin lights blinked back on and hundreds of people yawned and stretched in unison. Holly squinted at me and smiled. "Are we there yet?"

Yeesh.

We landed in Guangzhou with China still cloaked in darkness.

Turns out that it was 5:40 a.m., March 29, 2018.

We'd skipped a day.

UPON EXITING THE GIANT PLANE, WE WERE HERDED into lines at the immigration check-in, one for foreigners and one for nationals. So far, China was exactly how I pictured it — stark, gray, and humorless. The gate agents all wore military-like uniforms and friendly customer service was clearly not high on anyone's priority list. Efficiency was, though, and we were quickly ushered through that line, up an escalator, and into another cue. This was the security part, complete with more stern agents, some real soldiers standing by, and a plethora of video cameras. Again, frowning people requested our passports and boarding passes. We emptied the contents of our backpacks into plastic containers to be scanned.

An agent made me open the tiny-guitar-shaped case that held my camera gimbal. "What??" she demanded, pointing at the device.

"Camera gimbal!" I shouted at her as if she was hard of hearing, making descriptive gestures and nodding my head furiously, the internationally recognized symbol for "this guy is a doofus." She rolled her eyes and motioned me through.

After we gathered our belongings, yet another agent demanded to see our passports again. *We're not in Kansas anymore,* I thought.

We soon exited the Scary-Overly-Paranoid-Communist-Military-State portion of the airport and entered the See-How-Nice-And-Modern-We-Are area. Though not quite measuring up to the

International Terminal at LAX, it was quite beautiful, and the excitement of actually being in China was powerful.

As soon as possible, we sat down and initiated the process of connecting to WiFi, not that we're addicted to technology or anything. The sky outside had begun to lighten, and although appropriately overcast and rainy outside, we finally had an idea of the time of day.

I should say, our watches and phones now knew, but our bodies were fast becoming confused. It seemed that we had just settled into our airport seats when the flight to Kathmandu was called. This was another China Southern flight, but on a smaller plane, not the Airbus 380 — the largest commercial jet on Earth.

It was fun while it lasted, but I was pleased to be leaving China. I made a mental note that I someday need to venture out into the Chinese countryside and experience the better parts of this country, not just the gray, humorless, and governmental parts.

ANOTHER MATCHING SET OF ADORABLE FLIGHT attendants welcomed us as we boarded, and we found our seats, this time near the front of the plane. Although it was now light outside, one of the attendants motioned for me to close the window shade, which I found strange. What didn't she want me to see out there?

We took off into the slate gray Chinese sky. This time, Holly had the common decency to stay awake and keep me occupied for the first thirteen minutes, which was an improvement. At minute fourteen, she was propped against my shoulder and out cold.

Four hours passed in a blur of Netflix documentaries, vain attempts to stretch my legs under the seat in front of me, and additional weird dreams filled with white noise. During wakeful times, the thought of freeing my trapped legs and putting them to work on a Himalayan trail was intoxicating, but seemed so far away.

Again the nose of the plane tipped downward as we began our

descent into the Kathmandu Valley. In defiance of the flight attendant, I pulled up the window shade and spent the last thirty minutes staring out the window at the changing landscape.

At one point I was able to look across the cabin and see through the window of another rebel passenger on the other side of the plane. It became clear that what I first perceived to be clouds were actually snow-covered mountains. Rats! We were sitting on the wrong side of the airplane to see the Himalayas now clearly visible in the distance.

We would be seeing them much closer very soon.

My view wasn't bad, though. I could make out what appeared to be terraced, agricultural land and shorter mountains until homes began appearing in increasing numbers, then multi-story structures, then a LOT of them. Suddenly, we were flying over the outer perimeter of the city and the horizon became a smoggy blur of earth-tone buildings.

Kathmandu!

The size of the city was incomprehensible for a small-town boy like myself. As the plane descended to land, we could clearly see the incredible crush of humanity and motor vehicles on the streets below.

Then the buildings were rushing past as we approached the runway.

Screech! We touched down.

Just like that, twenty-three hours of cramped legs, crazy dreams, android-like flight attendants, middle of the night meals, marathon movie binging, and a Twilight Zone space/time continuum was over. Just outside the window of the airplane was Nepal, that mysterious place we'd been working to see for so long.

It was 10:40 a.m., March 29, 2018.

We were here.

TWO

NAVIGATING THUNDERDOME

On legs shaking with both excitement and fatigue, Holly and I descended a covered staircase from the airplane to the tarmac of Kathmandu's Tribhuvan International Airport. The whine of jet engines, the dieseling of shuttle buses, and the chattering of a hundred excited passengers created a cacophony that nearly overpowered the sound of Bob Seger singing "Ka-ka-ka-ka-ka-ka KAT-MAN-DOO!" in my head.

But not quite.

Holly and I climbed aboard a packed shuttle bus and each grabbed a dangling hand strap as the vehicle lurched forward. After a very brief trip, we all piled off the bus and headed en mass toward the entrance to the immigration lounge of the airport, pausing long enough to snap some quick pictures. Like a herd of bleating lambs, we pushed and shoved each other into the lounge, also known as Thunderdome.

At this point, previous knowledge won out over ignorant enthusiasm, and we fell into the latter designation. Those passengers "in the know" made a mad dash to a collection of round wooden tables and writing surfaces that were affixed to the walls.

This is where the immigration forms were and in the blink of an eye, every available writing utensil and table space was snapped up like seven blind puppies fighting over six teats.

After the initial shock wore off, Holly and I tried to appear somewhat competent (which didn't matter because no one was looking at us) and sidled up to the first table that had any space. Suddenly throwing elbows like the enforcer of some backstreet roller derby team, my sweet wife battered her way into the space and snatched up a pencil and a fistful of forms before an equally tough Indian woman could reach them.

Holly points out where we are, as if we needed any reminding at this point. Photo by the author.

We retreated to a clear desk, hunkering over our fresh kill of immigration documents like snarling wolves. I attempted to fill out my forms myself, but my normal form-filling-out anxiety kicked in and I ended up just waiting for Holly to finish so I could copy hers. After she admonished me for entering my social security number into the flight information boxes, I fixed the mistake and we moved to the next group of lines to which people seemed to be migrating. A single plastic sign above read "Without Visa." We had no visa, so it made sense.

Thus began the waiting that, as the late great Tom Petty points out repeatedly, is the hardest part. We waited and waited, inching forward when possible, and filling the time with awkward small talk because it was impossible to concentrate on any single thought. Swaying from foot to foot is popular during these types of waits, I've noticed. Looking over the anxious crowd of foreigners, the entire room seemed to be swaying and shifting in place, like a sea urchin undulating beneath an ocean current. Clearly, everyone was either anxious or really needed to pee; probably both.

Finally, it was our turn to approach the immigration officer, and we did so confidently, forms in hand.

"Where is your visa receipt?" he asked bluntly.

"Um, don't we get that here?" Holly responded. I stood back, hoping he wouldn't ask me any hard questions, like my name.

"No, you need to get it over there!" he said, clearly annoyed. He pointed to the other side of the room where there was a set of three equally long lines. "You purchase your visa there and then come back here with the receipt. You can come straight to the front."

WE HAD WAITED IN THE WRONG LINE FOR FORTY-FIVE minutes. Now we had to start over again.

We took our places at the back of one of the lines, speculating about which one of the three was correct. It was really a crapshoot because at the front of each cue were random signs displaying convoluted messaging regarding strange combinations of acceptable currencies. Above the entire set of lines was a large sign advertising a local bank that also, in tiny lettering, read "Visa Fee Collection Counter." It felt as if that the Head Gamemaker from the Hunger Games had been put in charge of this place and that the passengers would soon be wantonly slaughtering each other in a desperate effort to survive.

After another forty minutes, we made it to the front and by dumb luck were able to purchase the correct visas. Then, it was back to the "Without Visa" line, which no longer made any sense, but okay. We brazenly strutted to the front.

Actually, it wasn't brazen at all. We kind of slunk to the front.

As a proper, born-and-bred Southerner, jumping to the front of any line was unthinkable for me. I could feel the wrath of dozens of scowling eyes on me, so I turned and began apologizing profusely to the grumbling people. Thankfully, the immigration agent called us forward and quickly processed our forms before the crowd could take revenge. We grabbed our passports and scampered away.

We would now locate our bags and escape relatively unscathed. That was the plan, at least. We approached the baggage area and spotted our stuff: one suitcase, two Hobnail bags, and five large duffels packed with the new sneakers we would distribute via the Shuzz Foundation. I grabbed a metal luggage cart and loaded it full, heading for the exit in triumph. I could make out the welcoming Kathmandu sunshine streaming through the exit doors just a hundred feet away.

Suddenly, another immigration officer leaped out of the shadows and cut us off. "Excuse me, sir? These bags must be x-rayed!" He was referring to the Shuzz duffels, each of which had been affixed with a large red tag that clearly translated to "SWARM, SWARM!" The unsmiling man directed us to a large x-ray machine and motioned me to put the bags on the conveyor. I did so and the bags moved through as several agents stared at the computer screen, frowning and murmuring to each other.

"Can you open the bags, please?" one agent asked as the duffels exited the machine. I unzipped one, revealing the sneakers. "Why do you have these?! What are these for?!" he demanded.

Trying to remain calm, I explained that they were part of a charitable effort and I quickly produced the Shuzz documentation.

"How much are these worth?" he shot back, ignoring the documents.

"I have no idea, sir. We are giving them away, not selling them."

By now, more agents had gathered around, frowning and murmuring to one another. The Main Guy finally decided that his best course of action was to take the paperwork and disappear down a hallway for an approximate eternity, leaving us standing there surrounded by bags. As we waited, novels were written in their entirety. Boys grew into old men and passed away peacefully of old age. I was concerned that the Himalayas might actually erode down to nothing by the time we were allowed to leave the airport.

Finally, the Main Guy reappeared and we all agreed that the sneakers would be held hostage in the airport until our Sherpas could come back and pay ransom for them, probably tomorrow. Yes, you read that correctly. The sneakers that we had brought from the other side of the planet to GIVE AWAY TO CHILDREN IN NEED would be held hostage in the airport and would require bribe money to be released. Under the glare of suspicion, the agents finally allowed us leave. It was approximately three hours since we had walked into Tribhuvan Airport/Thunderdome/The Hunger Games.

WE STUMBLED OUT OF THE AIRPORT AND INTO THE blinding sunlight of Kathmandu. Immediately, a chorus of voices began shouting at us, vying for our attention. "Taxi here! Cab here! Sir, please! I help you now!" Before we could register any of these requests, I heard the distinct and friendly voice of Dawa Jangbu Lama Sherpa, our trek leader, call out my name above the cacophony.

We spotted our friend shoving his way through the mass of taxi drivers. In his hand, he held a sign displaying our company name. I've never been so happy to see a person *or* a logo.

After exchanging bear hugs with Dawa, Holly and I followed closely behind as he led us through a tangle of people and small vehicles parked at crazy angles in the parking lot. Some guy who I assumed was with Dawa grabbed my bag out of my hand and carried it the short distance to our vehicle. He bluntly demanded a tip when we arrived at the car. Before I could respond, Dawa chastised the man in angry Nepali and motioned him away.

"Yeah, what HE said!" I shouted at the man, flashing an awkward gang sign.

Holly and I piled into the relative security of the car's back seat; Dawa and the driver, a handsome young man, got into the front seats. Somehow, perhaps by black magic, the driver was able to insert our vehicle into the flow of what could only be described as an angry hornet's nest of buzzing, honking, shouting, contorting, but somehow miraculously moving sea of all manner of humanity and vehicles that spilled into the city streets of Kathmandu. Holly and I gripped any available surface of the car with white knuckles, certain that we'd never make the hotel alive.

However, a clearly thrilled Dawa put our minds at ease.

"You've made the trip all the way from the U.S.," he said. "Now, my guys will take over. Just relax and don't worry about anything."

THREE
REALLY, REALLY WHERE I'M GOING TO

There are some moments in life that just don't seem real at all.

We knew that it wasn't a dream and we were actually in Kathmandu, Nepal, but it sure wasn't registering. Holly and I were absolutely dumbfounded yet thrilled.

It was mid-afternoon on Friday, March 29, and we were in a country that, until now, was the place in "Raiders of the Lost Ark" where Nazi-fighting Indiana Jones found Marion in her Himalayan bar, beating the local Sherpas at their drinking games. To a fifteen-year-old farm boy from North Carolina, no place on *earth* ever seemed as exotic, dangerous, and romantic as Nepal. And here we were.

Traffic in Kathmandu consisted of hundreds of thousands of cars, scooters, motorcycles, horse-drawn carriages, human-powered rickshaws, cattle, people, and dogs all doing their own thing as quickly as possible. The general rule seemed to be that whoever got to the empty space first had claim to it. Only the largest intersections contained traffic cops, and nobody seemed to be paying much attention to them.

I was certain that we would witness a fatal accident at any moment. A large truck approached us in the opposite direction and I was horrified to see a motorcyclist overtake the vehicle and duck in front of it just as we passed, avoiding disaster by mere inches. We zoomed past pedestrians so close I could have reached out and pushed them out of the way. Six "lanes" of traffic rushed around a cow that had decided the middle of the road was a good place to lie down.

(Note: As Nepal is largely Hindu, cows are considered sacred and must not be killed. However, male calves are routinely turned out into the city due to their inability to produce milk. Dawa is a volunteer at a non-profit that collects these orphans and cares for them until their natural deaths.)

The thrill ride ended as we turned down an alarmingly narrow side alley and pulled up to our accommodations, Hotel Tibet.

A young doorman rushed out as we rolled to a stop. As I stepped out of the vehicle, he folded his hands and greeted me with a genuine "Namaste," the first of hundreds we would give and receive over the next three weeks. I learned over time to say it in singsong fashion: *Nama-stayyyyyy.*

WE ENTERED THROUGH THE GOLD-PLATE FRONT DOORS into a main lobby elegant in gold, red, and yellow. A low ceiling, wood floor, and collection of well-worn couches gave it a luxurious yet homey feel.

A slender young Nepali man approached me. Before Dawa could introduce us, I recognized him by his enormous smile and boyish shock of black hair along with his Hobnail Trekking shirt and cap. It was Tenzi, our senior guide.

"Namaste, sir!" he practically shouted, grabbing my hand and shaking it wildly. "Welcome to Nepal!"

"Tenzi, you have no idea how much we've wanted to meet you!" I said. "And now, we're finally here!"

"Yes! Now we can become friends!" He punctuated the

sentence with an uproarious laugh, enunciating each individual "ha" into a cartoon version of exaggerated merriment. But it was genuine and incredibly contagious, and within seconds, everyone in the room was in stitches without knowing why. Thus his nickname: "HaHa Tenzi."

Dawa seated us on the couches as Tenzi placed white and yellow sacred scarves around our necks while the front-desk clerk presented us with small glasses of tasty mango juice. This ceremonial welcome made us feel like royalty.

"You guys can take your time, relax, and explore the hotel," said Dawa in his perfect, elegant English as we sipped our drinks. "There is a money exchange place just around the corner from here, and you can also do some shopping if you like. Let's plan on getting together for dinner tonight at around seven."

Dawa then presented us a skeleton room key that was attached to a heavy plate with the hotel logo and our room number engraved into it. We grabbed our bags, wedged ourselves into the narrowest elevator I've ever seen, and slowly ascended to the fourth floor.

We found our room at the end of the hall. The skeleton key worked perfectly and we entered a room conventionally furnished with a king-sized bed, TV, desk, and a couple of chairs.

The first thing we noticed was that there was no electricity in the room. We tried all the toggle switches — there were a bunch of them located in odd places throughout — but nothing happened. I sat on the edge of the bed and called the front desk to inquire.

"Yes sir, you must turn on the power switch on the wall outside the front door," the clerk instructed.

There was, in fact, another toggle switch on the hallway wall outside the room. I flipped it and the room hummed to life. I opened the windows to let in the 72-degree breeze and looked over the city. Our view was mainly of the rooftops of nearby buildings, many of which featured large black-plastic water tanks. A light brown haze hung over the city and the honking horns and engine noises were punctuated with an ever-present rattling of jackhammers, some near and some in the distance, as Kathmandu continued to resurrect herself after the devastating earthquake of April 25, 2015.

I collapsed on the bed, ready for a serious nap, but Holly was having none of it.

"C'mon, let's go get something to eat!" she urged. "They said something about a rooftop restaurant."

Foiled again. I dragged myself off the bed and tried to match Holly's well-rested exuberance as we headed up to the restaurant.

The Yeti Bar & Terrace, situated on a charming little deck appointed with potted plants and prayer flags, offered a great view of the city and overlooked a surprisingly large and modern Radisson resort hotel across the street.

For some reason, I didn't expect a Radisson here, but that just showed my ignorance. It wouldn't be the only time.

The restaurant was straight up awesome. It was nice to be in the open air after spending the last twenty-four hours in the bottled environment of airplanes and airports, even if Kathmandu's atmosphere was dangerous to breathe. We didn't notice any obvious pollution so we didn't wear buffs or masks — probably not a great idea.

After enjoying our first Nepalese meal consisting of ice-cold, sweaty bottles of Everest beer, chicken momos (Asian steamed dumplings), and fried yak-cheese fingers, we made the short hike to the money exchange shop. The place was about the size of a large phone booth (for those of you who still remember them) and was not air-conditioned, which made the quarters a little close and uncomfortable for my taste. But the proprietor was a pleasant, well-dressed guy who quickly pointed out that he had been in business for twenty-seven years and also owned two shops across the street. I guess trust is a big deal when you're a moneychanger.

The process of changing our U.S. dollars into Nepalese rupees was easier than I expected, mainly because I work under the assumption that everything will be a disaster. Flush with Nepalese moolah, we skulked back to the hotel like drug dealers, suspicious of anyone who approached within fifty feet. Clearly, we weren't used to carrying cash money and I was relieved to be back in the room where we could stash our zillions of rupees safely away.

We devoted the rest of the afternoon to becoming unconscious as quickly as possible.

At around seven, Holly and I shook off the nap cobwebs and made our way down to the hotel restaurant where we hooked up with the first of our thirteen trekkers: childhood buddies Luis Prieto and Mike Maxim, and a family friend, Stefanie Ruman. Our conversation consisted mainly of two topics: Number 1: Can you believe we're actually in Nepal? and Number 2: Holy crap! Can you believe we're actually in Nepal?!

Holly had developed a post-flight headache, so after confirming that we were actually in Nepal, we called it quits. Even after an absurd marathon of too much activity and too little sleep, I still found it difficult to drift off.

I AWOKE TO A STRANGE COMBINATION OF SOUNDS: A jackhammer, creaking footsteps in the ceiling, and the hoarse squawking of a weird bird on our windowsill. It sounded like a bird version of the actor Harvey Fierstein. (I never pinpointed the species, but we encountered the croaking bird several times along the trek. It was large and black, like a crow. In fact, it was probably a crow.)

I got up and showered. The bathroom was nice, fully tiled, but odd. The shower area shared the same floor but was separated from the vanity area by a clear piece of Plexiglas that was only about half as wide as it should've been. This resulted in me spraying water all over everything during the course of the shower, soaking the entire bathroom. Halfway through I realized that I was allowing water to get into my mouth. I immediately began spitting it out wildly, trying to remove every microscopic contaminant. A recurring theme when traveling to faraway places, I've noticed, is a constant soul bartering with both God and the Devil (covering both bases) in exchange for an ironclad guarantee of no dysentery. It rarely works, but I was hoping.

We headed down to meet others for breakfast in the lobby restaurant. From a distance, the spread looked very similar to an American buffet, with breads and pastries displayed on serving trays and the heated fare covered under shiny metal, roll-top chafers. (I had to Google "metal buffet serving thing" because who knows what that is actually called? Now we both know.)

Famished and excited to get my bacon, eggs, sausage, and grits on, I uncovered the first chafer to reveal . . . something. I perceived it to be some type of fried meat, possibly fish. I suspiciously put a few of whatever it was on my plate and moved to the next chafer, convinced that the first was just an anomaly.

Vegetables, perhaps eggplant.

Onto the next.

Rice.

And finally…

Yeee-aahh, I'm not sure.

It was some combination of chickpeas, potatoes, onions, and other ingredients. I later found out this is collectively referred to as "takari. My dreams of a giant U.S.-style breakfast dashed, I sulked back to our table with my serving of mystery foods.

"I'm not sure about all this," I announced. "But I'm keeping an open mind."

Mike, who was almost finished, grinned at me.

"Dude, try the fish."

With a decidedly closed mind, I took a tiny bite of the fish and in a millisecond, an explosion of flavor coursed across my palate, busting open the gates of my mind.

This is actually good!

With the enthusiasm of Mikey discovering his Life cereal, I

gobbled up the rest of the fish and sampled the other stuff with much less suspicion. While not reaching the hero status of the fish, it was all perfectly edible. I quickly polished off my kid-size servings and went back, heaping the plate full.

While eating, we were joined by another member of the group, my childhood friend Jeff Campbell, whom I hadn't seen since my wedding over two decades ago. We now had matching St. Nicholas beards, but much to my annoyance, Jeff was clearly in better shape than me.

The plan for today was a temple tour that would include Swayambunath (commonly known as The Monkey Temple), Boudhanath, and Pashupatinath. This would take up most of the day, and we quickly talked Jeff into joining us. Mike opted to do some exploring on his own and catch up with us later.

Thirty minutes later, we were assembled in the lobby when Dawa walked in with another man, our tour guide, whose name was pronounced "Dee-Walker." To clarify the pronunciation, Dee-Walker suggested that we think of Luke Skywalker when saying his name. This created a problem, because I accidentally called him Dee-Skywalker at least twice, but he didn't seem to find any humor in my mistake.

FOUR

DON'T TOUCH THE MONKEY

A s we proceeded toward our first destination, The Monkey Temple, Dee-Walker launched into a clearly scripted but impressive monologue about the history of Kathmandu and the various buildings we were passing. The traffic somehow managed to thicken as we approached the temple, with taxis, trucks, and most of all, motorcycles swarming near the entrance. We could just make out the stupa — a dome-shaped structure and the most recognizable type of Buddhist shrine — high at the top of a hill. An incredibly long staircase led from the street all the way up, and we quickly spotted a few monkeys near the bottom.

"Do you want to walk up the steps or drive to the top?" Dee-Walker asked us collectively. In unison, we all responded with "Walk!" From the back of the vehicle, I heard Jeff's deep, deadpan voice say, "That's right. This isn't the Hobnail *Driving* Company, after all."

After the driver pulled over, we exited and made the treacherous journey across the street with a confident Dee-Walker leading us by using what I could only assume was the Jedi Mind Trick to stop traffic with one outstretched hand.

We snaked through a collection of beggars and flower vendors and began making our way slowly up the 365 steps that went straight to the top where the actual temple was located.

A variety of vendors solicited us as we climbed, mostly selling things like stone etchings, Buddhist singing bowls, animal carvings, jewelry, and various artwork. Holly and Stefanie were sucked in by the very first vendor, especially when he stated that we were getting the "morning price" and it would be more expensive later. Holly bit and purchased a "Namaste" etching for around $10 USD.

For the record, we encountered the "morning price" line from at least three other vendors on the way up. Sometime later, I overheard a vendor extolling the value of his "mid-to-late morning prices."

The higher we climbed, the more monkeys we encountered. There were baby monkeys, teenaged monkeys, and adult monkeys moving about, looking for something to eat. Some huddled quietly together in family groups while others — male adolescents, no doubt — ran amuck, tipping over trash cans, photobombing the selfies of unsuspecting tourists, and smoking monkey cigarettes while their moms weren't watching. They seemed to ignore the humans altogether except for when someone approached too closely. Then, they would lunge forward, feign attack with bared teeth, and scare the hell out of the person before scampering off.

The lesson? Don't touch the monkey.

We finally reached the top, well worth the climb. In addition to serving as an insane vantage point from which to view Kathmandu, the temple was a hodgepodge of sacred artifacts and structures, all surrounding the enormous stupa with very chill eyes peering out calmly in four directions. This was our first opportunity to do some serious prayer-wheel spinning, too.

I felt like a third-grader on a field trip as we followed Dee-Walker, who constantly had to round us up to keep us moving. I honestly wouldn't have been surprised if he'd distributed peanut butter and jelly sandwiches and juice boxes at some point. We exited the temple a different way and found our SUV and driver waiting for us.

An enormous crowd flows into the entrance to the Boudhanath. Photo by the author.

AFTER LEAVING THE MONKEYS, WE HEADED BACK INTO the thick of Kathmandu traffic. Twenty minutes of constant near-death experiences later, the driver pulled over to the curb and at Dee-Walker's direction, we piled out of the SUV.

A pulsating human river seemed to be flowing in and out of a wide alley between two buildings, and the five of us merged into this stream, careful to keep track of one another. As the stream turned into the alley, we were presented with a startling view: a gigantic stupa, much larger than the one at Swayambunath.

This was Boudhanath.

Practically yelling above the din of people, honking of horns, and a PA system blaring out Buddhist prayers, Dee-Walker told us that this temple dates back to 600 AD and is one of the world's largest spherical stupas. We happened to show up on a festival day, which accounted for the throngs of people, most of who were walking around both the base of the massive structure and further up, around the bottom of the dome in a clockwise direction.

We merged into the stream of people, eager to take part in the proceedings but having no clue what we were doing. Before we could make a full circuit, our guide ducked into the doorway of one of the many buildings facing inward toward the stupa. We followed and climbed a flight of stairs that terminated at the doors of a wood-fired pizza restaurant, the obvious choice when dining in Kathmandu, right?

We found seats on an open-air terrace that overlooked the Boudhanath, ordered our pizzas, and sipped cold beers. The combination of Eastern religion and Western-influenced dining made for a strange dichotomy, and again, I had an out-of-body sense of time and space. I had to keep reminding myself of where I was, but I wasn't sure I believed myself.

Just before the food arrived, in strolled our fellow trekker Mike Maxim, whom we'd last seen at breakfast at the hotel.

"How in the world did you ever find us?" I asked him, amazed.

"I used a map," he said with a shrug. "No big deal. I knew the name of the restaurant."

Any other member of our group — and I'm referring to myself — would have immediately curled into a fetal position and shut down all systems had we been left to our own devices in this city.

But Mike is seasoned traveler, a literal rocket scientist, and is built like a Marvel Comics superhero, so people tend not to mess with him. Peppering him with questions concerning his survival, we polished off our Nepali pizza while watching the activity below.

"OK, let's go!" shouted Dee-Walker, ushering us out.

We re-entered the flow around the stupa. I assumed that we were headed toward the exit. Suddenly, Dee-Walker veered off into another doorway and motioned us to follow. He led us up a flight of steps into what appeared to be some type of art gallery where two or three men were sitting cross-legged on the floor, painting canvases.

"I thought you would want to see this mandala gallery," explained Dee-Walker. "We won't stay here long."

Apparently, the word "won't" can also mean "will" in the Nepali culture.

More than an hour later, after a young man recited for us an exhaustive history of mandala painting, we were hit with the hard sell. "We are offering you good prices," our group was assured. Much later, we found out that Dee-Walker was in cahoots with the art gallery and would receive kickbacks from any sales made from his tour groups. When Dawa caught wind of this he was furious, and that day would prove to be the end of the line for Dee-Walker and Hobnail Trekking.

OUR LAST TEMPLE WAS A DEPARTURE FROM THE FIRST two. Although they were both very sacred sites, both Swayambunath and Boudhanath also had a bit more of a tourist angle. Pashupatinath however, was the real thing.

We had to walk a little way to get to the temple, and we immediately noticed that there were more beggars here. Before, we were being solicited by what essentially amounted to street vendors carrying actual merchandise, but now we were walking past some of the most incredible poverty I've ever seen. These people were either very old, horribly disabled, or some combination of both. It was clear that they lived on the street.

Dawa had instructed us at the hotel that under no circumstance should we give money to beggars while in Kathmandu, so we didn't, but it was difficult here.

Dee-Walker paid our temple fees and we entered through a stone archway. As a Christian who is accustomed to churches, I guess I've always pictured temples as single buildings. But these Hindu and Buddhist temples tended to be more than a single building. Pashupatinath is a huge complex of structures that have been built up over time around a single two-story pagoda, situated along the sacred Bagmati River.

After crossing the river via a large stone bridge, we encountered three Hindu *sadhus*, or holy men, gathered around the front of a small stone structure. Although I knew in my logical mind that these were extremely devout and spiritual men, it was hard to look at them and not be reminded of very laid-back hippies. They sported brightly colored, simple clothing and sandals, painted faces, and very long beards dyed (or painted) to match their color schemes, like ZZ Top Easter eggs. They were smiling, friendly, and lounging in a way that felt like stoners hanging out on somebody's couch. I halfway expected to hear "Uncle John's Band" playing in the background.

I say this with only the best of intentions and greatest respect.

AFTER AN EMOTIONALLY OVERWHELMED HOLLY WAS blessed by the sadhus, we took a seat on a stone ledge that overlooked the river and the cremation rituals that were happening. This is a daily occurrence at the temple and mandatory in the Hindu religion. Every day, dozens of dead bodies are cremated here quite visibly on a pyre of wood and greenery. The event is solemn and quite shocking for Westerners, and frankly, it felt a bit weird and inappropriate to be watching it like a sporting event. Soon,

Dee-Walker was moving us along. Though fascinated by it, I wasn't sad to leave Pashupatinath.

Holly is overwhelmed by the incredibly cool process of being blessed by the sadhus. Photo by the author.

We arrived back at the hotel to find the rest of the Hobnail group had made it in from the airport, and most were still in the lobby. It was a grand reunion with people who had become great friends over the past six months during our many training hikes and Facebook posts. It was amazing to me that fifteen of us had come from different places across the U.S. and had managed to end up at the same hotel in Kathmandu at precisely the agreed-upon time.

Yet it is impossible for the Johnsons, who all live in the same house, to get to church on time. Ever. But I digress.

A couple hours later, those of us who weren't too exhausted from travel met for a group dinner at a nearby restaurant that also featured traditional Nepali and Sherpa dancing. The dancers boogied down as we slogged our way through course after course of delectable Nepali fare, more than we could possibly eat.

I found it hard to concentrate on the stage show knowing that in just a few short hours, we would be heading to the airport for our flight to Lukla and the start of our trek. As much as I had enjoyed my first two days in Kathmandu, I was anxious to get my boots on the trail. It was finally time to see if all those miles of hiking and training had been enough.

But first, we had to survive the flight and subsequent landing at the World's Most Dangerous Airport.

FIVE

HEY, DID YOU HAPPEN TO SEE THE MOST DANGEROUS AIRPORT IN THE WORLD?

S leep came in fits and starts. I was having one dream after another of waking up to find that we'd overslept and missed the entire trek, stuff like that. When the alarm finally went off at 4 a.m., I sprang out of bed. We gathered our belongings and within thirty minutes, were in the lobby with the rest of our groggy but excited group.

While the Sherpas carried our duffels out and stowed them on top of several vehicles, Dawa divided us into travel groups. Holly and I were in the first vehicle, an SUV. As I climbed into the front seat holding my backpack, I noticed something that nearly stopped my heart: my GoPro was missing from the gimbal.

"Oh, fuuuuuddddgggggeeee." Only I didn't say fudge. (*A Christmas Story*, 1984)

Only ten minutes before, in the room, I had inserted the small action camera into the gimbal's foam rubber clamps and put the whole thing in a side pocket of my backpack, but now the GoPro was gone.

I leapt out of the vehicle, ran back into the hotel and up the stairs to the fourth floor, and then sprinted down the hallway, which kept stretching out longer and longer like in a horror movie. My leaden legs struggled to reach the end.

There was the GoPro, on the floor outside the room.

I nearly wept from a combination of relief and mortification. The brand-new Hero 5 had almost been lost before recording a single moment of the trek.

Holly would've killed me.

I scooped it up and sprinted back to the SUV. In five minutes, we were on our way through the darkened, nearly empty streets of Kathmandu and I was breathing again.

OUR CONVOY OF THREE VEHICLES ENTERED THE AIRPORT through the "Internal Flights" entrance and we off-loaded, everyone double-checking to make sure they had their gear. Then we followed Dawa and Tenzi through the security protocol and into the small gate area where the Sherpas handed us our Summit Airlines tickets.

"Be ready," Dawa advised, explaining that the pilots would fly as soon as they were given the green light by the officials in Lukla. "They might call us at any time, so expect to leave quickly."

Tenzi and Hari, another member of the Sherpa team, distributed boxed breakfasts containing a banana, two boiled eggs, cheese toast, an apple, and a box of mango juice. There was also half a sandwich that appeared to contain a pink, creamlike, mystery jelly. No clue.

But I was too excited to either eat or sit down and filmed a little with my iPhone as others in our group began opening their boxes. Suddenly, Tenzi's voice rang out.

"Yes, they are ready for us! Follow me, please!"

We hadn't been there five minutes.

In a mad rush, people began grabbing backpacks, food boxes, and boarding passes while scrambling to keep up with Tenzi, who was leading us past the gate agent at a brisk trot. For a moment, it was chaos. A yeti could've taken my boarding pass stub and I wouldn't have noticed.

We followed Tenzi through a tunnel and onto the tarmac where several shuttle buses sat idling.

"It's this one!" he shouted, and we began boarding the bus like D-Day Airborne Division soldiers piling out of an airplane over Normandy, but in reverse. Just as the last trekker squeezed on, we heard a loud voice.

"No, it's THIS one!" shouted Dawa, still on the tarmac and pointing at another bus.

We all turned, de-boarded the first bus, and ran to the second.

A chorus of giggles rose throughout the group as the absurdity of everything began to overtake us. I was sure that we would leave at least one member of the team behind, perhaps unwittingly flying to Siberia, but after a quick but careful roll call, Dawa accounted for everyone just as the bus lurched forward.

We raced down the tarmac at breakneck speed (well, like thirty miles per hour) and squeaked to a stop near a collection of Summit Airlines planes. One of them seemed to be the center of attention and Dawa shouted back at us, "That's our plane!"

After a pause, they motioned us to come and for the fourth time in about three minutes, we got off or on another vehicle.

Holly and I were first in line at the plane, and a young flight attendant welcomed us aboard with a "Namaste" and directed us to the front.

For some reason, she made one of our trekkers, sixty-one-year-old South Carolinian, Kathy, sit next to her in the back. It made no sense, but whatever.

Soon, the plane was full with our group — fifteen trekkers and three Sherpas. Two more Sherpas would meet us in Lukla.

The fuselage of the LET 410 Turbolet aircraft was fairly crackling with excitement as we buckled in. The engines roared to life and we cheered. A few minutes later, the scotch blocks were pulled away, the brakes released, and the plane began moving forward.

And we cheered.

At this point, any discernible movement of the airplane short of a catastrophic explosion would elicit a wild hoorah from the group, such was our anticipation.

The plane turned onto the runway, paused for a moment, and then sprang forward at full power. The wheels left the ground and we were off to more crazed cheering, swooping over Kathmandu as golden sunlight began peeking over the distant mountains.

FLYING NORTHEAST FROM THE CITY, THE GROUP settled into a melody of oohs and ahhs as we progressed past better and better vistas underneath. Soon, the snow-dusted peaks of the Himalayas began appearing on the horizon, but unlike the flight into Kathmandu from China, this airplane was heading straight for them. We began passing uncomfortably close over snowy ridges and past sheer stone cliffs. I became aware that we were flying between mountains rather than over them.

The 45-minute flight seemed more like five. About halfway through, Dawa called out that we were flying over his village of Junbesi, and pointed out his family's house, the blue metal roof clearly visible on a hillside. Amazing.

Then, the tipping downward of the aircraft's nose announced that touchdown was coming. GoPros and smart phones all filming furiously, the terraced farms, homes, and teahouses of Lukla rushed upward to meet us, speeding past as we crossed over the drop-off at the end of the runway by mere feet.

The back wheels bumped down and the eighteen-person trekking team became drunken soccer fans as their squad scored to win the World Cup. Never have I heard such exultation from airplane passengers.

AS SOON AS THE WHEELS ROLLED TO A STOP, THE

ground crew pulled the door open and we disembarked the craft. A cool, crisp wind struck us as we stepped out and I made a mental note that the 75-degree temps of Kathmandu were now over. This was proper Himalayan air and I could feel the coldness rush into my lungs.

Holding our caps against the prop-blast of the plane's propellers, we followed Tenzi across the tarmac, through a chain-link fence, and into a lodge, Everest Mountain Home. The building was so close to the tarmac, I could literally still hear the engines of our plane as we took seats in our very first teahouse.

Then, Dawa moved ceremonially to the center of the room.

"Welcome to Lukla and the beginning of your trek!" he said with a broad smile. "It's time for the fun to begin!"

Raucous cheers...

"You can finish your breakfast, enjoy a hot cup of tea, and finish any shoppings you might have," he said, adding an "s" on the end of shopping as is his custom. "Please be ready to start walking in about an hour."

Then, Dawa made formal introductions of our Sherpa team, which now included Phurba, a friendly, athletic man in his mid-thirties, I estimated, and Ngwang, our "yak man" whose age was indeterminable. He was tiny and slim with a more Tibetan look to his face than Phurba's. He gave us a shy smile and said "Welcome to Nepal" in a nasally, high-pitched but pleasant voice.

Every one of us Americans struggled with the pronunciation of both Ngwang's and Phurba's names. It was several days before I was brave enough to try addressing them by their actual names rather than "Hey man" or "Hey buddy" or "Hey ultra-cool super-human Sherpa dude."

After downing our teas, Holly, Jeff, and I walked into the village to handle our last minute "shoppings" by purchasing an extra set of sunglasses, some toilet paper, and lip balm. We then rejoined the group in time to load up, give our backpack straps one final adjustment, and exit the lodge in single file.

. . .

AT THIS POINT, I FEEL AS THOUGH I SHOULD INTRODUCE you to the trekking team, as they constituted the inaugural group of Hobnail Trekking Co. This was a big deal for Holly and me because no matter how many ways you look at it, these nuts. . . I mean lovely people, had placed their very lives in our as yet untested hands in a remote country halfway around the world. This was either an amazing leap of faith or a spasm of insanity.

So, in order of when they registered . . .

First was my aforementioned friend, Jeff Campbell, 53, with whom I attended high school in the North Carolina mountains back in the early '80s. Jeff is all mountain man, a strapping 6'4" beast with a white beard and Sam Elliott-deep voice. A longtime national park ranger, Jeff later launched his own business satellite-mapping huge tracts of forestland for various clients. He was definitely the most qualified outdoorsman of our group, and his dry, deadpan humor always appeared when least expected.

Kathy Jones, 61, is a slim, elfish lady from St. Simons Island, Georgia. Quickly appointed "Trail Mom" by the group, Kathy was always smiling and never appeared to be in any distress whatsoever. In fact, as someone twice her size and 9 years her junior, I was routinely embarrassed at how well Kathy performed in comparison with myself, so I was forced to step-up my game or look foolish. The latter is what usually happened.

Kathy's daughter, Rachel Bishop, 34, also from St. Simons, was the first of two physician's assistants to join the group. She and her mom made a formidable and seasoned adventuring team, having knocked out Mt. Kilimanjaro the previous year. Rachel had suffered acute mountain sickness on that trek, so she was on a mission to complete EBC without a problem. She was a constant source of both medical prowess and inspiration. (Spoiler alert: she made it there and back, no AMS at all!)

Shari Seaman, 36, from Franklin, Tennessee, was the other

physician's assistant and served as the Bad Influence of the mini-group that included Kathy, Rachel, and Gina Gage, whom I'll get to in a minute. It was Shari who talked the others into this fine mess after attending a Hobnail presentation a year earlier. I considered Shari to be the heart of our team, always ready with a booming laugh and words of encouragement. I also found it disquieting that Shari's specialty as a PA is helping end-stage patients with pain management. Was this coincidence? I secretly prayed that her skills wouldn't be required on this trip.

Gina Gage, 33, rounded out the St. Simons-based group. An unlikely warrior as tiny as Ngwang, Gina, a striking blond, always flashed her broad smile and never complained, even when afflicted with stomach problems for several days before and after Base Camp. She made us Big Tough Men look like pansies.

Next came a married couple, Russ, 53, and Susan Moore, 52, from Tuscaloosa, Alabama. Enthusiasm personified, Russ, a professional in the financial industry, is a former University of Alabama cheerleader, and Susan is a gymnastics instructor. The two, also both Crossfit instructors, compete in dozens of obstacle races every year and haven't missed a single Crimson Tide football game since 1984. Insanely fit, the Moores brought constant levity, positivity, and excitement to the team. Russ would even encourage every pack animal we encountered.

"Way to go, buddy! You're doing great!" he would say to the confused yaks, who only speak Nepali.

Steve Tudor, 61, from Nashville, is a tall, slim Renaissance Man. A widower and father of a two college-age daughters, Steve lives life as fully as anyone I've ever met. An avid snowboarder, pilot, scuba diver, and marathoner, he is also a highly accomplished skydiver and makes many jumps each year, usually filming others with his camera equipment. A storyteller extraordinaire, Steve kept the group fascinated and in stitches throughout. He was also dubbed "Trail Dad."

Luis Prieto, 36, also a Nashville resident, is another adventure nut. An athletic banking industry professional, Luis is an avid scuba diver, equestrian polo player, and board member of the Shuzz Foundation, a non-profit that delivers new shoes to children in areas of natural disasters and such. Always ready with a word of encouragement, Luis added yet another super-charged boost of energy and confidence to the group.

Stefanie Ruman, 45, of Murfreesboro, Tennessee, has been a friend of our family since she and Holly began doing Crossfit together in 2010. A petite, athletic woman, Stef's contagious smile was ever-present, as was her distinctive giggle and wicked sense of comic timing. A self-proclaimed "details freak," it nearly took an act of Congress to convince Stef to take the plunge and register for the trip, but once there, she was all in.

Mike Maxim, 35, of Los Angeles inadvertently made the rest of us guys look like buffoons (not difficult in my case). But as one of the most polite people I've ever met, I'm sure he didn't mean to make us all (me) look like loser slobs. By all accounts, Mike is the Perfect Human. He's brilliant — a senior rocket engineer for Elon Musk's company, SpaceX; a seasoned traveler with more than two dozen countries checked off his list; a former University of Florida cheerleader; and is a competition salsa dancer. In a word, he's disgusting. Mike came on board to trek with his childhood buddy, Luis. By the end, he was a lifelong friend to us all.

Speaking of childhood buddies, Bill Shupp, 46, of South San Francisco, California, grew up in McLean, Virginia and attended elementary school with Holly. He is now an accomplished drummer and veteran of several rock bands, a computer programmer, and an extraordinary photographer. Bill joined our squad as an opportunity to photograph the epic landscapes of the Himalayas. Even burdened with heavy camera gear, he was one of the strongest hikers of the team. Check out Bill's photography website at shupp.com.

The last to register was Natalie Bethune, 41, of Franklin, Tennessee. She had decided to pull the trigger on the trip after joining one of our group training hikes back in January. A health care industry professional, Natalie is a seasoned world traveler and was a consistent calming influence on a party that otherwise tended to bounce off the walls. Natalie developed a sinus infection early in the trek but powered through without a complaint, yet another inspirational figure for me. I'm particularly proud of the fact that without knowing a soul in our group beforehand, Natalie is now "besties" with several of the ladies.

A quick word about my do-gooder wife, Holly, that she would probably prefer I not mention. But since I'm The Author of this book, I get to say what I want.

It was Holly, some eight years ago or so, who decided to change her life by entering a Biggest Loser competition at her workplace. In making this commitment (she won, by the way), Holly discovered Crossfit and set into action an indirect course of events that would eventually lead to this trip.

Two years ago, she began to have serious problems with both her shoulders and knees, resulting in surgeries on all of the above except for one knee. The last surgery, the repair of a torn meniscus in her right knee, came in October 2017, just six months prior to our departure to Big E. More than half of those remaining months were occupied with physical therapy, and it was only in January that Holly was cleared to train in earnest. But there was only so much she could do.

Finally, during an appointment one day in February, Holly's orthopedic surgeon, Dr. Michael Pagnani, tried to talk her out of going. I did, too. If I recall correctly, her initial response was, and I quote:

"*&%$#$%!!&^$%@#*%, I'm going!!"

After taking a few hours to relax and think through what we were saying, remembering that our suggestions were made purely out of love, Holly sat me down at home, face to face, and said:

"*&%$#$%!!&^$%@#*%, I'm going!!"

Okie dokie. I guess that answered *that* question.

She trained for about a month, received a strategic cortisone shot from the doc, and climbed aboard the airplane. On paper, Holly had no business undertaking such an adventure, but she would not be denied.

I was hoping this wouldn't come back to bite her.

The Hobnail group, preparing to depart Lukla, had no idea what was in store at the moment this photo was made. First row, from left: Dawa, Mike Maxim, Kathy Jones, Tenzi, and Bill Shupp. Second row, from left: The author, Holly, Stefanie Ruman, Rachel Bishop, Gina Gage, and Jeff Campbell. Third row, from left: Russ Moore, Susan Moore, Steve Tudor, Luis Prieto, Natalie Bethune (below Luis), and Shari Seaman. Photo by Mike Maxim.

SIX

BOOTS ON THE GROUND

In no particular order, the fifteen of us — plus five Sherpa guides and four yak/cow hybrids called dzos — headed through the village of Lukla and onto the EBC trail.

The village itself is fairly expansive, consisting of teahouses, shops, and residences, all on a relatively level plateau. We walked down the "main drag" of the place on a wide, stone-laid street as shopkeepers and children took casual notice. It's not that they weren't used to seeing trekkers, but our group was larger than most.

Upon walking through the archway exit/entrance of the village, we immediately began heading steadily down, with Tenzi setting the pace and Dawa bringing up the rear.

There was constant chatter with the most prevalent subject matter being "Can you believe we're finally doing this?" The weather was spectacular: temps in the mid-50s and a brilliant blue sky with scattered clouds along the tops of the nearby peaks. It seemed incomprehensible that the mountains would get higher than these.

They would. A lot higher.

And so would we, although for the first leg of our trip, we lost over six hundred feet of altitude. I couldn't help thinking, *Jeez, climbing back up into Lukla twelve days from now is going to absolutely suck.*

Within the first few minutes, we passed both our first porters and livestock trains. The porter, a single guy, was coming up the first slope upon our leaving Lukla, carrying what appeared to be a heavy load. Because this was our first encounter with a porter in action, we all stood and gawked. I'm sure he appreciated our gawking.

Same thing with the animals, in this case, dzos. We had all seen them countless times on video, but real life is different. As the clanking bells approached, I was nearly moved to tears by the excitement of seeing real (kind of) yaks in Nepal. They, on the other hand, couldn't have given a rat's butt about seeing me.

Before long, we approached our first suspension bridge, and it was an impressive one. For anyone with a fear of heights, the pucker factor was strong right off the bat. The bridge was stretched over what appeared to be an old landslide where a large section of the mountain had sloughed off, resulting in a giant, impassable wound filled with boulders and debris, probably a hundred feet below. Most of us were awkward on the bridge at first, lurching this way and that as the structure swayed, squeaked, and vibrated. I was near the front, and after crossing, filmed other members as they completed the task.

"The first of many!" I remarked to Tenzi, who responded with "Yeah, yeah!" and broke into peals of laughter, flashing a mouthful of blindingly white teeth.

I never realized I was so funny. I was practically Don Rickles and never knew it.

The trail wound up and down alongside the Dudh Kosi River, a rushing torrent of aquamarine glacial water that originated at the Khumbu Glacier. This river would be a nearly constant companion for the first several days of trekking, with its white-noise roar either increasing or decreasing in volume depending on how close we were.

We also passed through one village after another, all with teahouses, tables set up with Sherpa merchandise for sale, and children playing in the trail and peering out of windows. The villages would come and go so quickly, I never knew most of their names.

As we walked, I noticed that Jeff had become quiet and contemplative. I asked him if he was okay.

"I'm just thinking about Nick," he said, referring to his college-age son who is also an outdoorsman. His first semester of college had prevented him from joining his dad.

"I just wish we had found a way for him to come on this trip," Jeff said. "Now that I'm here, I regret not making that happen. He would be so blown away by this landscape."

We continued down the trail in silence for a while.

AFTER AN HOUR-LONG STOP FOR A LUNCH OF GARLIC soup and Tibetan bread (like a flat, round, bread pancake) at Mt. Kusum Garden Restaurant & Lodge in a village called Thadekoshi, we continued toward our destination for the day, Phakding. At some point after lunch, I began thinking to myself, *Dang, shouldn't we have gotten there by now? Wasn't this supposed to be the easy day? Stop! Turn around! You're heading away from civilization, not toward it!*

Ah, the survival instinct, she is strong.

At around 2 p.m., we finally arrived in Phakding. It would become a recurring theme during our ascent that, with one or two exceptions, our teahouses always seemed to be at the upper end of the villages. So our excitement at arriving in a destination village was soon dashed when we realized we had to still climb to the top of it before reaching sanctuary. Such was the case here.

But arrive we did, following our Sherpa leaders into the comfortable common room of the Namaste Lodge.

"Congratulations on your first day!" said Dawa, applauding for us. We all cheered and high-fived. While everyone else was looking the other way, I crumpled into a corner chair.

Tenzi and Hari began making the rounds to take our tea orders. Standard choices throughout the trek were black, lemon, ginger, and mint. Here we learned that while on trek, our Sherpas were also our waiters. Upon entering a teahouse for breaks or meals, the guys would move from guide mode to waiter mode, communicating orders to the on-site kitchen staff (usually the owners and residents), serving the food and drink, and staying on-call for refills or any other needs. After the meals, one of the guys would usually walk around with a notepad and take orders for the next meal.

As we enjoyed the tea, Tenzi called out room assignments and handed us our keys. Excited to see our first teahouse bedroom, Holly and I grabbed our backpacks and headed that way. As we left, Dawa reminded us that the shoe distribution event would begin outside in two hours.

Our room was quaint and comfortable, with one queen bed and a private bathroom. We unpacked our sleeping bags, rolled them out, and jumped in for a test run, just to rest our legs for a few minutes.

Or not.

The next thing I knew, I woke with a start to the sounds of screaming and laughing children, clueless about where I was. Slowly, my consciousness returned.

Beside me, Holly was snoring.

I grabbed my phone to check the time: 4:30. We had completely zonked out and the shoe distribution was well underway. Mortified, I threw on my boots, grabbed my camera gimbal with the GoPro, and left Holly asleep. Reflexively, I shut the door lock on the outside of the door.

There was a huge crowd of locals and their children near the teahouse entrance, and clearly the shoes had all been given out.

The kids, each with their own race bib provided by Steve's Nashville-based running club, were now engaged in boys and girls short sprint races through the street of Phakding. I managed to film the last two races.

As I walked back to our room, the last one at the end of the building, I heard pounding on the door.

It was Holly, locked inside our room by nap-groggy me. She had been trying to get someone's attention for the past twenty minutes, but couldn't be heard over the screaming and laughter of the children.

Oops. I opened the door sheepishly.

"Did you have a good nap, Sweetie?"

This room at our teahouse in Phakding was representative of all of them. Small and cozy. Photo by Rachel Bishop.

We reconvened in the common room for dinner. Veggies and rice were on the menu for me. As we finished up, Dawa briefed us on what to expect tomorrow.

It had been an incredible first day, yet Holly and I both felt a slight sense of dread over what the next day might bring. As excited as we were to experience the village of Namche Bazaar, everything I'd read and heard suggested that the hike to the village was not for the faint of heart.

Nevertheless, we were excited — about everything. The food, the room, our new gear — it was all exciting — and to be honest, I wasn't sure I'd be able to sleep at all.

Silly boy.

I BECAME AWARE OF LIGHT IN THE ROOM AND reluctantly opened my eyes.

It was April 1, Easter Sunday.

The glow of the bright red, flower-print curtains suggested a clear morning. From my sleeping bag, I reached out and moved them aside, revealing a vista that had been covered by clouds yesterday. We were in a valley far below a snow-topped massif — a single, wide mountain with multiple peaks.

Crazy.

I lay snug in my bag, my brain and my bladder in a death match over who would win the "Should I go to the bathroom now?" debate.

The question was settled when I heard voices outside our door followed by a gentle knock.

"Good morning! Tea!"

I opened the door and there stood Hari, holding a pitcher, and Phurba with a platter of tea glasses.

"Namaste!" they both cried in unison, wearing huge smiles.

"Namaste!"

"Would you like sugar in your tea?"

"Yes, please. Only a little in mine, please. Just dump the whole bag into Holly's."

My wife smiled with her sleepy face at the Sherpas.

"Namaste!" she croaked at them.

"Namaste!" they shouted back.

I carried the steaming glasses to the bed.

This is how every morning began. Returning to the States two weeks later, we would become despondent upon realizing that we had to wake ourselves up with no smiling faces and steaming beverages at our door.

For now, though, we enjoyed our teas and pees.

Thirty minutes later, we left our Hobnail duffels outside our room as directed and met the group in the common room where Tenzi, Hari, and Phurba were already carrying hot plates of food out of the kitchen.

Hari, left, and Phurba greeted all of us sleepy trekkers with hot tea each morning. Photo by Rachel Bishop.

"Who had muesli with raisins?"

"Who had a veggie omelet?"

"Who had hard-boiled eggs?

"Who had Tibetan bread?"

Soon, we were all hunched over our plates. Upon conducting a casual poll, I found that almost everyone except Jeff had slept like logs the previous night. Turns out that Jeff suffers from fairly severe sleep apnea and, due to the lack of consistent electricity in teahouse rooms, had opted not to bring his CPAP machine.

"I'll deal with it," he told me over breakfast. "It's just one of those annoyances I have to put up with when I go camping."

A new little seed of worry planted itself in the back of my brain. I hoped it wouldn't grow.

After finishing breakfast, the process of preparing our packs for the day's hike began, which mainly involved replenishing snacks and filtered water. For those with hydration bladders in their packs, this involved filling them with bottled water or H^2O that we had treated ourselves. Most of us used some combination of a Steripen, iodine tablets, and/or tap water that the kitchen staff had boiled for us the night before. Holly and a few other people also had a LifeStraw filter bottle that, in theory, worked perfectly fine on its own, though we always used two methods.

Incidentally, I had left Nashville with a LifeStraw bottle, too, in one of the side pockets of my pack. By the time we reached China, it was gone.

I paid $43 for it. Never used it once.

Doofus Dad, indeed. It bothered me for the entire trip. Still does.

Soon, Dawa had us all together outside the common room entrance and ready to go. Our four dzos stood by, staring at us impassively, as Ngwang strapped the black Hobnail Trekking Co. duffel bags on their capable backs.

"Please gather around," said Dawa. He gave us a shy smile. "If it's OK, I'd like to ask a prayer for our safe journey."

Among trekking groups, it was highly unusual for Sherpas to be a part of Christian prayers because of the general dominance of the Buddhist religion in the Himalayas, but Dawa had converted to Christianity a few years ago. It had never been discussed, but clearly, everyone in our group seemed eager to participate. We formed a circle as Dawa offered a quiet prayer for our health, the care of our families at home, and the success of our day's hike, as well as a few words regarding Easter.

"Amen!"

We shouted the word in unison with the same enthusiasm that had been displayed upon landing at Lukla. Dawa was clearly thrilled, and religious or not, this launched a very challenging day for us mere mortals in the best possible way.

The Hobnail group lit out.

SEVEN

THE MOTHER OF ALL HIKES

A cool, brilliant morning greeted us as we hiked out of Phakding and into the rocky wilderness. The only sounds were those of our conversation, waking birds, and the ever-present roar of the Dudh Kosi. We traveled through stone-wall-lined farmland, thick pine forests, and tiny villages. We crossed more bridges spanning wide sections of the river.

As would become our habit in the mornings, Dawa and I hung back and discussed the positives and negatives of the trek thus far. There were only positives.

"Except for locking me in the room yesterday!" Holly, apparently eavesdropping, yelled back at us.

As the sun rose higher, another common sound — the low chatter of helicopters — began. This became normal, and after a few days, I began measuring our elevation by where we were in relation to the choppers. It was startling to see them flying through the valleys far *below* us, but this would come later.

Our morning tea stop was in the hamlet of Benkar. Most of these picturesque villages were built on terraced levels with stone staircases running through the middle, making these sections some of the most grueling to hike. The lodges and residences (usually one and the same) were built of wood frames, stone siding, and tin roofs, often up to four stories. Brightly painted window frames added a pop of color. Storefronts built alongside the trail were always open with the smiling proprietor displaying the exact same bottled waters, candy bars, buffs, beanies, tubes of lip balm, and other trekking supplies that every other storefront offered. Although it detracted slightly from the remote feel of the trek, we were nonetheless happy to have access to these conveniences.

In one village, just before a river crossing, we came upon a small, one-story stucco building where our dzos were "parked" out front. A small sign affixed to the building read "Welcome Ngwang Friendship Tea Shop." I didn't realize that this was actually Ngwang's home until the trek back, when he invited all of us inside for tea.

We continued past the house and expansive, back-yard vegetable garden, and over a long suspension bridge that crossed the river immediately behind the Sherpa's house.

What a place to live!

In Monjo where we would stay for our last night on trek, lunch was at Mt. Kailash Lodge . I decided on dal bhat and it was a wise choice.

Make that absolutely awesome.

Dal bhat is the staple meal of the Sherpa people, often eaten once or even twice a day, every day — essentially the Nepali equivalent of mac and cheese for American kids.

Compared to mac and cheese, though, dal bhat is healthy, the perfect combination of protein and carbs for the physical requirements of hiking or working at high altitudes. It usually consists of lentil soup (dal) and steamed rice (bhat). Beyond that, it is supplemented with some combination of curried potatoes, pickled vegetables, some type of greens, and takari. In teahouses lower down, you may get a little of all of these, but the higher you go, the less complicated the plate becomes. It's always insanely tasty, though.

Lunch finished, we continued, soon reaching the entrance to Sagarmatha National Park and UNESCO World Heritage Site. After Dawa handled our entrance fees and paperwork, we walked through a large, concrete structure painted with Buddhist artwork, spinning a row of several prayer wheels. As if to say, "OK, buddy, now it gets real," the park trail immediately dropped into a steep descent, plunging into a gorge. The route then began to vary wildly from steep, dusty woodland sections to wide open bottomland alongside the Dudh Kosi that were so filled with rounded, eroded stones, stable footing was nearly impossible.

After several minutes on one of these sections, we rounded a bend and spotted in the distance the famous Hillary Suspension Bridge, its twin counterpart offset below. After looking at this iconic sight in photos and videos for nearly two years, to see it in person was surreal, as if I had inserted myself into a YouTube video, like Jeff Bridges in the movie "Tron."

Except he had those cool, laser motorcycles to ride. We had to hoof it.

After a ten-minute rest, we ascended a steep incline to reach the bridge, which required another breather as we readied our GoPros and iPhones for the monumental crossing of this icon.

In my mind, I was also making last-minute, back-room deals with God Almighty. If this bridge decided to break, it was going to be a long, scary drop to Eternity, and I wanted to make sure my prayer payments were not past due.

Across we went, me with my camera gimbal in one hand, filming with my GoPro. Similar to our landing at Lukla, the nearness to certain death created an other-worldly exhilaration. We were so high, hanging between two mountains, that if felt as if we were in a helicopter minus the flying part. Although I was never actually scared, I have to admit that the solid terra firma felt good under my boots when I made it to the other side.

Another milestone completed. It was a watershed moment for two reasons: the iconic crossing itself, and the fact that we would now embark on the most brutal, ass-kicking part of the hike, perhaps of the entire trek.

The Hillary Bridge below Namche Bazaar was, at once, exciting and horrifying to cross. Photo by Mike Maxim.

WITHOUT APOLOGY, THE TRAIL IMMEDIATELY ENTERED A pine forest and began a snakelike switchback pattern straight up a mountain, so steep and never-ending that I lost sight of the tiny, ant-sized trekkers far above us. Here came the mental toughness part. We slowed to a snail's pace, staring down at our feet in front of us, plodding one step at a time, switchback after switchback.

Adding to the difficulty was the constant flow of mules, porters, dzos, and other trekkers either passing in the same direction or going the other way. In either case, we had to stop and find space to move off, which on paper, sounds like a good thing. In reality, it breaks your momentum and extends the misery. The animals also kicked up clouds of dust as this section was mostly powdery soil and yak dung pulverized by the constant pounding of boots and hooves.

Jagged roots stuck out now and then, just to keep things interesting.

After an hour or so, we reached a plateau where an impressive bathroom structure and stone seating had been built. We took a ten-minute break here and snacked on energy gummies and beans, trail mix, and candy bars. Jeff and I took a few minutes to check out the species of flora and quiz Dawa on the indigenous wildlife.

"When do we get to see a yeti?" is what we were really getting at.

Back to the grind, and it was more of the same. At some point, I looked back down the trail and realized to my amazement that the Hillary Bridge was just a speck far below, and I could hardly hear the river at all. Although our pace seemed agonizingly slow, we had actually progressed much farther than it felt. I was also newly aware of a shortness of breath, announcing the effects of altitude.

Up, up, up.

IT WASN'T A CONSCIOUS DECISION, BUT I ALMOST NEVER looked at the time while on the trail. Much like the airplane flight to China, the time of day became a nebulous concept. All that really mattered was avoiding injury or sickness, staying hydrated, and trying to live in the moment, whether that moment was good or bad. Each day was calculated by the east-to-west arc of the sun and by our successful progress to the next village, but the moments were measured by the memories that were being filed into the filing cabinets in our brains. This incredible vista, this painful step, that funny comment.

The "N" cabinet was bursting at the seams and it was only Day 2.

Properly filing the memories was more difficult than you would think; my brain would often throw up its figurative hands and important moments would just drift to the floor. It seems that placing yourself into such exotic, extreme, and unfamiliar surroundings creates a new set of problems for your brain to deal with. This is why, I believe, the oft-uttered comment "I can't believe I'm here" was actually a literal statement. The speaker really *couldn't* believe it. The brain was flummoxed.

Consequently, photography is critical in these situations. The little 2-gig memory card is an unbiased participant and dutifully records whatever scene the camera's sensor sends it. It isn't influenced by emotion or experience or whether the photographer is a doofus. Weeks, months, and years later, we can review these photos and videos, see ourselves, and be reminded that it actually did happen. There I was! I have proof!

Up, up, up.

And then I became aware that the trail was leveling slightly and I looked up, afraid that it was only an illusion. Before me, the switchbacks had ended and the trail had resumed a posture of gentle curves and slopes. We were over the worst of it.

SUDDENLY, I HEARD WHOOPS AHEAD. AS WE ROUNDED A bend, the mysterious, multi-colored, insanely terraced village of Namche Bazaar appeared through the trees, still high above us. Adrenaline kicked in, pushing us on.

We entered the village quite literally by walking through the entrance pagoda, painted in gaudy reds and golds. A large, ornate, viaduct system ran alongside the trail (which had become a walkway of inlaid stones) with a steady stream of gravity-driven water powering enormous spinning prayer wheels that had been built into the system. It was almost like something you'd see at Disney World or on the Vegas Strip, but this was quite real. Even as a Christian, I was comforted by the idea that these wheels were flinging thousands of Buddhist prayers into the atmosphere like drops of water from a radial sprinkler.

I hoped some of them were for me.

The ornate prayer-wheel viaduct system at Namche Bazaar is mind boggling. Photo by the author.

At first, I was so blown away by the viaduct and various pagodas, it didn't register that we were climbing a very steep and absurdly long set of irregular steps that led into the heart of Namche. After another five minutes or so, it began registering.

Even on the most brutal sections of the day's trail, we had the benefit of switchbacks to give our legs and lungs small respites, but the Namche staircase was having none of that. It went straight up, punishing us for having the gall to arrive here.

"Sure, you might have made it here," the village seemed to say with a menacing laugh. "But you haven't made it to your teahouse yet!"

Our teahouse, of course, was near the top.

We trudged, gasping, through the 11,000-foot-high village, winding past dozens of shops, restaurants, and bakeries, and passing one enticing teahouse after another. Inside, we could clearly see happy trekkers relaxing, enjoying beverages, smiling, and pointing at us out the window.

More teahouses passed.

"Is it this one?"

"No."

"Is this it?"

"Nope."

"Please, God, is THIS it??"

"No! Sorry!"

Eventually Tenzi hung a right down an alley and we saw our lodge, Green Tara. Hoarse cheers went up, weak high fives were smacked, and pitiful fist bumps were exploded.

We walked in and, as one final insidious insult, were forced to climb two flights of stairs to reach the common room, where we collapsed in dusty, shivering, sweaty, exhausted heaps.

Actually, that was just me. Everyone else was fine.

Reaching Namche was one of my proudest accomplishments, and we hadn't even seen Mt. Everest yet.

. . .

THE TEMPERATURE RARELY BOTHERED ME WHILE trekking, even during the coldest days at altitude. It was when we stopped walking that the problems kicked in. Although our Merino wool layers were lifesavers and kept us relatively dry, it was impossible not to sweat at least some, so it was a constant effort to regulate our body temperature when at rest. We were going to get chilled, no matter what.

That's where the hot tea came into play. At Green Tara, we drank it slowly, savoring the heat as it warmed our cores.

The common room was a large one, with tables lining the perimeter and several in the middle of the room as well. One wall had the cashier counter where you could purchase candy bars, WiFi cards, charge your electronic devices, or pay for other services. Beside that was a pass-thru to the kitchen through which the Sherpas would pick up meals as they were ready. It was a cozy place.

After our room assignments and keys were distributed, Dawa told us that our rooms had private bathrooms and even showers, but he had no guarantees on how long the hot water would last.

"The water is heated daily by solar energy, and when it's gone, it's gone," he explained. "So if you want a hot shower, you'd better hur..."

There was a scurry of boots and banging noises as chairs were tipped over backward and people bumped into each other. In a flash, at least half the room — including my wife — had disappeared down the steps, fumbling with their room keys as they ran, yanking off layers of clothing. It looked like the opening sequence from "Hard Day's Night" when screaming fans were chasing the Beatles through the streets of Liverpool.

"Geez, these people are ridiculous," I commented to a startled German man seated next to me. "You'd think they'd never had a hot shower before."

Inwardly, I cursed at myself for not choosing a seat nearer to the stairs.

. . .

I LINGERED FOR A WHILE IN THE WARM COMMON ROOM, sipping tea and typing up my trip notes for the day on my iPad using a connected Bluetooth keyboard.

This must make me appear impressive, I told myself, like a big-time journalist writing a story for **Outside** *magazine or something.*

When I glanced up to see all the impressed people, nobody was looking.

Dang.

I enjoyed listening to the conversations going on around me. Almost every voice I could hear was either speaking English in a non-American accent or speaking another language altogether. This was truly an international adventure, and no matter where the trekkers and climbers were from, we were all able to commiserate with each other. The brutal trail to EBC was a great equalizer — no one was immune to the challenges, regardless of their level of fitness.

After a while, I packed up my stuff and headed to our first-floor room, hunched over to keep from bumping my head on the ceiling as I descended the stairs. Clearly, Nepal was not used to accommodating 6'5" guys.

When I walked into our room, Holly was exiting the bathroom, already dressed in her fleece jammies, face red and shiny, steam billowing out from the door behind.

"Ahh, yes," she purred. "That was lovely! I feel a hundred percent better. Now to snuggle into the sleeping bag until dinner."

I was already peeling off my clothes and headed for the vacated shower. I opened the hot water faucet all the way and stood there naked in the rapidly cooling bathroom, jabbing at the water with my fingertips to test the temperature.

It's not getting hot.

Please!

Nope. Not gonna happen.

Dejected, I re-dressed and crawled into my sleeping bag, jealous of Holly's cleanness.

After a short nap, we headed upstairs to dinner with the group. Even after such a taxing day, the Hobnail team was in high spirits and our loud laughter drew disapproving glances from other tables. But we'd earned it.

Dinner for me was Sherpa stew, a staple found at every teahouse with slight alterations. Most of the time, it contained garlic, potatoes, carrots, and cabbage. Depending on the teahouse, flat noodles, dumplings, spinach, and different spices could be in there as well. Regardless, it was always piping hot and really hit the spot, especially with a piece of Tibetan bread.

After dinner and Dawa's briefing, several members of our team got a card game up. I hovered around the perimeter of the table, and upon realizing that "Go Fish" wasn't on the docket, I slumped away and down the stairs.

I had other work to do, anyway.

As a photojournalist and communications pro in my former life, I had grown accustomed to documenting and photographing trips, and this was no different. I knew that for Hobnail Trekking Co. to become successful, I would have to generate as much proprietary creative content as I possibly could, mainly in the form of photos and videos. We had worked out an arrangement with Bill Shupp to handle the lion's share of the still photography on the trip, so I focused on shooting as much GoPro footage as possible. Part of my nightly routine was preparing my memory cards and above all, making sure all my extra batteries were charged.

Exciting, eh?

Our wonderful teahouse in Namche featured working electrical outlets in all the rooms, so my goal was to keep my iPad, iPhone, all four GoPro batteries, and my ZeroLemon high-capacity power bank fully charged. Frankly, I lived in terror that just as a yeti loped across the trail in front of us, my GoPro battery would run out.

YETI: *Hi there, Mr. Trekker! Here, let me just pause dramatically, framed perfectly by Mt. Everest itself in the background, so you can shoot crystal clear, HD video of me and become rich and famous. Ready?*

GOPRO: BEEP, BEEP, BEEP!

ME: Crap! OK, can you wait there long enough for me to change my GoPro battery?

YETI: Y'know … nah … never mind. I'll catch the next guy. See ya! (Bounds away.)

These were the kind of nightmares that kept me up at night.

I spent an hour simply downloading data, deleting extra footage, and plugging things in. After turning out the overhead light, the room glowed like a house of ill repute with all those little red "Charging" indicators on my electronics. I had to cover them up with socks and buffs just to darken the room enough to sleep.

Holly, of course, was oblivious to this. She had already completed enough of her puzzle book to get sleepy and konk out.

I climbed into my bag and lay there for an hour, wondering how I got to where I was. Imagine — an old Carolina country boy like me in a place like this!

Who'd a'thunk it?

EIGHT

THE ONE BESIDE THE BIG, POOFY CLOUD

After our morning wake-up tea and a hot muesli breakfast, we gathered outside the front entrance of Green Tara Lodge in final preparation for our "rest day" acclimatization hike. Climbing into higher altitudes would allow our flatlander bodies to adjust and prepare by manufacturing more red blood cells than we normally carry in our system, compensating for the lowered density of oxygen in the air. More red blood cells would essentially have our bodies working overtime to supply oxygen to our muscles and organs, thus allowing us to go into places where we really shouldn't go.

The local Sherpas are naturally set up this way. The rest of us losers have to work at it.

The plan was to hike up the mountain above Namche, have tea at the Everest View Hotel — about 2,000 feet higher than our current location — then descend into the village of Khumjung for lunch and a visit to the monastery there that contains the famous yeti scalp.

After double-checking our water and snack supplies, we gathered in a circle for Jeff to say a prayer. After one final gear check,

Tenzi started us out with an enthusiastic "Joom, joom," the Nepali equivalent of the more familiar English version — "Zoom, zoom" — made famous in old Mazda commercials.

The remaining incline of the insidious Namche staircase lay in wait for us. Inside of thirty seconds, the jovial mood that permeated the team quickly drained away and the conversation quieted, replaced with a fifteen-person choir gasping in unison up the uneven steps. After ten minutes, Hari, who was leading, waved us to a stop.

"Let's take a breather," he said, clearly not needing one.

I looked around, mortified. We were *still in the freaking village.* Children were gawking at us out of shop windows, wondering what our problem was. This staircase was trying to kill us all.

As one, team members began dropping their packs and peeling off the layers they had just meticulously donned. Then we were back at it again after a short rest and the staircase merged into a dusty trail on a flat plateau.

Here the trail forked — one way heading right, a lovely level path bending around some sloping mountainsides, and the other way headed straight up, daring us to attempt it at our own peril.

Guess which way we went?

Hari apologetically explained that tomorrow, when we continued to our next destination, we would take the level trail, but today was about acclimatization.

"SOME 'REST DAY,'" I MUTTERED UNDER MY BREATH. Tenzi caught my complaint and broke into a peal of exaggerated laughter because, clearly, I was joking. I nodded enthusiastically and laughed back at him, adding a string of silent keyboard symbols into my unspoken sentence.

Up, up, up we went.

This was similar to the ascent to Namche, but the switchbacks were sharper and we had climbed out of the forest. Now the trail meandered through low, scrubby bushes, affording us much better views. Again, the weather was spectacular and the snow-dusted, high peaks surrounding us were unearthly. In fact, the views were so beautiful, they kept distracting me from lamenting my lack of fitness.

Why, oh why, didn't you start training earlier and work harder? I would moan to myself. *If only you had hiked four days a week instead of three!*

My only solace was that, as I looked around, everyone seemed to be struggling, even people much younger and thinner. It occurred to me that we had officially arrived at High Altitude Central, and the work of manufacturing all those extra red blood cells must be well underway. This is what we had signed up for, and frankly, no amount of Stairmaster workouts could have saved us from getting schooled like this.

That said, I was concerned about Holly. She seemed to be getting the worst of it, and it was no real surprise because of her abbreviated training time. Just to make it possible for her to hike on her bad knees, she was taking multiple pain medications, wearing braces on both legs, and now, she was dealing with cardio issues on top of that.

Several times, Holly had to stop to take extra breaks, letting others walk past. All of our team was worried about her, offering words of encouragement.

Tenzi, however, had the perfect thing to say.

"Yeah, yeah, it's okay," he told Holly in his choppy, accented English. "Slowly, slowly catches the monkey."

This elicited a hearty laugh from both of us. It was a phrase that I grew to love, especially when the Sherpas replaced "monkey" with "yeti."

An hour later, the trail suddenly leveled and widened. We were atop a ridge, the trail lined with wind-ravaged evergreens. We came around a bend and there, strangely, was a teahouse lodge all by itself, surrounded by a dry-stack stone wall. Holly was a little ahead of me, talking to Dawa, as Jeff and I approached Phurba, who seemed to be waiting for us.

"Look there," he said, pointing to the horizon. "There is your first view of Everest."

For the past half hour, I had been so focused on Holly that I had barely looked up. Beyond the teahouse, the horizon was dominated by a collection of several enormous peaks, some layered behind others. Only one had a plume of snow blowing off the top. It was triangular, and at first seemed shorter than the others until I was able to perceive that it was actually farther away. Once I could make sense of the scale and distance, I realized that the triangular peak was actually gigantic.

I was looking at the world's tallest mountain with my own eyes.

There were no blowing trumpets, no fanfare, no confetti. Yet I felt disembodied, as if watching myself in a dream. It's impossible to prepare yourself for moments like these, and my feeble brain — which has enough trouble operating at normal altitudes — struggled to make sense of the vista.

The moment was just too monumental to process, so I didn't really try. It would have to be done later after time had passed. I have since interviewed several members of our group and asked them about their impressions of that moment, and they had similar responses. At the time, they tended to respond with the appropriate "Wow!" and "There it is! Unbelievable!" and continued on down the trail. But recalling it two months later, they were much more thoughtful and poignant, some actually weeping at the memory.

I thought of Chevy Chase's character, Clark Griswold, in "National Lampoon's Vacation" when he views the Grand Canyon for the first time. Griswold takes it in for three seconds and then hurries the wife and kids back to the Family Truckster, anxious to be on his way to Wally World.

We stood there for slightly longer than that while Jeff tried to point his finger to the peak so it would be distinguishable on my GoPro footage. We then continued to where Dawa was trying unsuccessfully to help Holly identify Big E from the other peaks.

"Is it the one beside the big, poofy cloud?"

"No, look to the right of that one."

"Oh, the one with the pointy place near the top?"

"No, you passed it. Move back to the left."

(Insert me rolling my eyes here.)

"Oh, oh, the little one with snow blowing off the top? Or are those clouds?"

"Yes, that's it," Dawa said, shooting me a sideways glance. "That's snow."

"OK, I see it. *Wow!* Look, honey! Mt. Everest!"

(More eye rolling.)

Holly admitted to me during the writing of this book that she *still* didn't know which one it was for the next thirty minutes, and was going around pointing out the wrong mountain to confused strangers.

Dawa decided to stop at the teahouse instead of continuing to Everest View Hotel for tea, which was the original plan. We enjoyed our hot tea with a front-row view of Everest (or in Holly's case, some other mountain) while visiting with a group of friendly Aussies. After a few group pictures, we were back on the trail.

THINGS GOT TOUGH AGAIN AS THE ROUTE ANGLED steeply upward for a long stretch before emptying onto a very cold and windy bald, a word we use in the Appalachian Mountains to describe rounded peaks with no trees.

Holly had had enough. The elevation, her knees, lungs, and now stomach were getting the best of her and she sat down on the ground, crying.

"Just give me a few minutes," she gasped. "I feel really bad."

Phurba trotted back to us and insisted that he carry Holly's pack for the rest of the day.

"Take your time," he said in broken English as he squatted beside her. "It's okay. Slowly, slowly catches the monkey."

I reminded her to think of the day's trek like a Crossfit WOD (workout of the day), which is what we normally did when faced with any tough challenge, physical or mental. As devoted Crossfitters for five years, this had become a custom for us. Five minutes later, she was ready to go.

In another hundred yards, we passed the steps leading up to the Everest View Hotel. The trail then began sloping downward into a sparse evergreen forest and heading into a valley that, until now, I had been entirely unaware of. In the valley floor sprawled a large village, distinctive in that every structure had a green tin roof. This was Khumjung.

Down, down, down. I could actually feel the increased oxygen as we descended, and I could tell this was helping Holly, too.

We stopped for a break at a pile of car-size boulders. As I sat on one, sucking water from my hydration tube, I happened to look down and noticed a pile of very old trash. Protruding from the pile was a piece of rusted metal that looked unusual. I pulled it out and discovered it was a long, curved blade, the handle of which had long-since eroded away or had been removed. Dawa said it was a Gurkha weapon called a "kukri" that would've been used to slash throats and accomplish other gruesome tasks like that. The blade still had an edge. An avid collector, Russ was excited about the find, so I happily gave it to him.

We continued through the village, walking between waist-high stone walls that also served as fencing for crops and livestock as well as the perfect surface for drying freshly washed clothes and blankets in the morning sun. Dozens of bright red, yellow, and orange shapes lay drying throughout the village like plashes of color in a Vincent van Gogh painting.

Near an elementary school established by Sir Edmund Hillary, we had lunch at yet another wonderful teahouse operated by a friendly, smiling family whose patriarch had summitted Everest multiple times. I had my best garlic soup with noodles to date.

Leaving our gear at the teahouse, we then walked across the village to the Khumjung Monastery, led the entire way by a fluffy, tail-wagging, black dog we nicknamed "KJ" in honor of his home village.

We got to the monastery, paid a small entrance fee, and entered, boots left at the door. In sock feet, we padded across a well-worn hardwood floor around the large, high-ceiling room. It was painted an amazing array of colors, primarily burgundy, yellow, and sky blue. On the right and left facing walls were hundreds of square cubbies containing Tibetan religious manuscripts. The back wall featured several large statues of Buddhist religious figures.

These were all beautifully painted and amazing to see, but the rock star was sitting on a small white pedestal in the center of the room. When I spotted it, an angel chorus sang in my head and gooseflesh popped on my arms.

THE YETI'S SCALP.

It was in a wood-framed, glass case, the top of which was fastened shut with a padlock. At first glance, the yeti's scalp looked like a shorter, wider, and hairy version of Dan Akroyd's noggin in the "Coneheads" skits on Saturday Night Live. I tried to give proper attention to the other neat things in the monastery, but Russ — a fellow Bigfoot enthusiast — and I essentially bee-lined straight to the scalp.

Since the fateful night in 1972 when my *incredibly* ill-informed parents took six-year-old me, along with my older brother and sister, to see "The Legend of Boggy Creek" at the Cardinal Theater in Raleigh, N.C., I've been fascinated by all things Bigfoot. The cult-classic, docu-horror film about an Arkansas Bigfoot-like creature thoroughly warped me to the point that I refused to stick my arm into the darkened bathroom to flip on the light when we got home. For years, I was convinced that Bigfoot was out to get *me*, specifically.

(Note: I had lobbied my brains out for the Mickey Mouse picture, "Fantasia," but was outvoted, 2 to 1. Had I won, I guess I might still be dealing with an irrational fear of mice instead of bigfeet. Hard to say.)

In high school, I began researching Bigfoot in earnest — checking out every library book I could find and watching all the television documentaries — and became acquainted with the Khumjung Monastery Yeti Scalp way back then. Truth be told, until years later, I was much more interested in the Yeti Scalp than I was in Mt. Everest or anything else about Nepal. I never became one of those crazy dudes you see on TV who spend all their free time actually searching for Bigfoot, but I sure love to watch those shows.

So encountering the relic in person was yet another watershed moment for me. Sure, it had been scientifically debunked some years ago, *supposedly* made out of the skin of a Nepalese mountain goat. Sure, it makes no sense that somebody found just the scalp, but not the rest of the head.

So what. Never let science and common sense get in the way of a good monster myth, I always say. As far as I was concerned, it was and always would be an actual yeti's scalp. We thoroughly documented the thing, spun a bunch of prayer wheels, and broke up a rip-roaring fight between KJ and some bully dog outside the monastery before making our way back across the village to the teahouse. Then it was time to ascend yet another imposing stone staircase that initiated the trail between Khumjung and Namche Bazaar.

At the top, we found a convenient rest spot — a level area with a white stone chorten (a stupa without the dome and eyes)– surrounded by low rock walls clearly built for seating. There were a few porters resting here, so Russ and Mike talked one of the young guys into letting them try out his load of tin roofing. With the load on their backs, supporting strap around their foreheads, the Americans, both very fit and strong, could barely get around the chorten once.

After a good laugh, the porter — probably all of 130 pounds soaking wet with his pockets full of nickels — reclaimed his load and continued down the trail like he was out for a Sunday walk, leaving the rest of us gawking.

The trail meandered over the ridge, past what Dawa described as the highest airstrip in the world, and eventually wound its way through a series of rocky switchbacks and down into Namche Bazaar. It was an off-the-beaten-path route that took us quite literally through the backyards of Namche residents, which was both cool and a little unsettling. I wasn't sure that I'd want strangers traipsing through my yard if I were them, but they didn't seem to mind.

| Namche Bazaar is best viewed from above. Amazing! Photo by Bill Shupp.

Nearing Green Tara Lodge, I had strategy on my mind.

As we approached the entrance, I rushed ahead of the group,

73

flung the door open, and sprinted down the hallway to our room. Once there— and with no thought for my lovely wife other than fear that she might beat me to it — I turned the hot-water faucet on full blast. I leaped under the steaming stream before anyone else could use up a molecule of that wonderfully warm goodness.

Aaaaaahhhhh. . . . .

Our group members spent the rest of the afternoon exploring the village, chilling out in the common room, or hibernating in their sleeping bags.

I slept well that night, sparkly clean and basking in the presence of all those new, microscopic oxygen warriors I had earned.

NINE

AN UNEXPECTED CONNECTION

I woke the next morning to banging noises coming down the hallway, along with voices speaking Nepali. I came to learn that days started very early in teahouses and that apparently, the Sherpa culture wasn't a very quiet one. On the contrary, it sounded like someone was moving a piano through the narrow hall, complete with loud, animated voices.

(In Nepalese) No, lift your side UP. UP!!

I am, but this doorway just isn't wide enough!

Stop, you're mashing my hand! Ouch, ouch, ouch!!

I burrowed deeper into my bag, wishing it was soundproof.

By the time Hari and Tenzi came around with morning tea, I had given up on sleep and was halfway packed. Holly was still snoring, impervious to outside stimuli.

"Honey, Brad Pitt brought you some tea," I whispered in her ear. She sat straight up. Works every time.

As much as we enjoyed our time in Namche, we were excited to move on and see what the next day's adventure would hold. After completing the hike from Phakding and surviving yesterday's acclimatization trek, we were flush with confidence. How much harder could it get, right?

We enjoyed a great breakfast in the common room (where I half expected to find a new piano), and gathered outside for the day's prayer. Then for the second consecutive day we tackled the infamous Namche staircase, although this time we were prepared for it, starting out with fewer layers and our circulatory systems teeming with additional red blood cells.

After a short break at the top of the staircase, smug as we watched other poor saps struggling up the acclimatization route we'd suffered yesterday, we took the level trail.

The next three hours or so would be some of the best on the entire trip. This trail was generally wide and level and seemed to be maintained by humans rather than forged by yak hooves. It followed the curves of the landscape, and each bend to the left— the conclusions of lengthy sections that followed the inward slope of the mountain — revealed a slightly closer and more impressive view of Everest than the last. Several of these bends began with a steep section of stone steps topped by a large, prayer flag-draped stupa overlooking the next section. The steps were always tough, but the trail tended to be level and forgiving.

The Dudh Kosi River cuts through a valley between Namche Bazaar and Tengboche. Photo by Bill Shupp.

We walked along in various, constantly changing pairings and sub-groups, discussing family, other hiking trips, and the like. This was a welcome change from the difficulties of the prior two days, when the uphill battles made conversation challenging at best and usually impossible. At one point, Dawa stopped me and pointed down the valley where it seemed as though we could see for a hundred miles.

"Look there, down below that low cloud," he said. "Can you see it?"

It was the Hillary Bridge. What had once seemed like an enormous structural marvel stretched high above a roaring river was now a dinky child's toy. From this height and distance, I couldn't even make out people on it. I realized how far we'd climbed and what a task we had already accomplished in only a couple of days.

We had just left one of the bends with a stupa when my phone began dinging, receiving incoming messages and texts. I jumped reflexively. It seemed that we had walked into a strong cell signal, a rarity here. The Nepali SIM card I'd installed the day we arrived in Kathmandu was finally working. I fumbled with the phone, excited by the prospect of having communication with the outside world because we hadn't been able to call the kids since leaving Lukla nor receive any information from them at all.

"Try calling Ava!" said Holly after we determined that it was around ten in the evening back home. "She'll still be up."

I dialed my daughter's cell number and after several rings, her sixteen-year-old voice answered with a confused "Hello?"

"Ava! It's Dad! Can you hear me??"

"Yes, I can! Hi, Dad! Oh my gosh! Where are you?"

"Mom and I are on the trail! I can't believe I've got you, honey. I'm actually looking at Mt. Everest right at this moment!"

It went on like this for several seconds, with me shouting into the phone. Afraid that I might lose the signal, I said a quick goodbye and handed the phone to Holly. She and Ava launched into a similar animated conversation.

As suddenly and unexpectedly as the cell signal had lit up my phone, a wave of powerful emotion washed over me as I watched Holly, a huge smile on her face, talk to our daughter. I guess the combination of our epic surroundings, the remoteness of it all, and the sheer distance home to our children was too much and I found myself nearly weeping. I tried to walk away and hide my face so as not to alarm the others, but Dawa spotted me.

"Is everything okay?" he asked. "Are the kids okay?"

"Yeah, they're fine," I croaked. "I . . . I . . . "

I couldn't speak anymore and only nodded. He put two and two together and gave me a bear hug (around my waist). "That's good, man," he said. "God is taking care of them. It's all good."

"Yep," was all I could get out.

After the call was over, we continued along the trail in silence, basking in the magnificence of our surroundings and reflecting on the blessings that were required to put us here.

An hour later, we rounded a curve and saw a small green table with a bright blue box on it, inscribed with white letters:

Donation Box

Namche to Tengboche

His Father and Grand Father

Ngundu / Lopsang Sherpa

A registration book secured by rocks was on the table as well.

Seated in a plastic chair behind the table was a very old man dressed in a threadbare green windbreaker, a bright red knit beanie with earflaps, and sunglasses.

This was the caretaker of the trail, which explained why this section seemed so well manicured. We had seen videos of this man for the past two years. I think Holly was more excited to see him than Everest. He was her version of the yeti's scalp.

She dropped in our donation, signed the book, and asked for a photo with old fellow. He was happy to oblige.

Just a few minutes later, we entered a small village and had our morning tea on the patio of the aptly named Ama Dablam View Lodge. We had picked up the cell signal again, so this time we were able to get Sam, our seventeen-year-old son, on the phone.

Apparently he was able to quickly silence the house party undoubtedly going on around him, which was impressive. Always calm, Sam talked to me about the ACT test he was taking the next day as if I was in the room with him, not in the Himalayas.

Also notable about this stop were the outside toilets, essentially a pod of outhouses at the end of the patio. Painted on the doors of the men's and women's facilities facing us were the words "Paid Toilets." I guess these were fancier, but I never found out because I chose the "Free Toilet" which was situated on the opposite side.

This is because I am "Cheap."

The toilet was essentially an outhouse with a rectangular hole cut in the floor under which was a large pile of leaves, compost, and other organic material. There was also a collection of the same organic material in the outhouse itself, along with a stack of dried yak dung. We encountered several of these types of outhouses and frankly, they smelled better than the "fancy" ones with plumbing. The Sherpa people had learned centuries ago that dirt, leaves, and even dried yak dung will keep the stink of fresh human waste to a minimum.

But enough about poop.

We left the village and started down into a gorge. Dawa had warned us during last night's briefing that we would have a fairly brutal ascent to Tengboche after lunch, so I recognized this as the opposite side. It was a knee-taxing descent and I could tell that Holly and Russ — who had undergone six knee surgeries over the past decade — were both having a tough time. Despite the slow pace, they remained in high spirits.

No worse for wear, we completed the descent and stopped for lunch at the Jambala Lodge and Restaurant, situated on the bank of the Dudh Kosi,. Just when I thought a bowl of garlic soup couldn't be improved upon, it seemed that the next teahouse topped it.

There are a lot of elements in a Himalayan trek that require mental adjustments, and diet tops the list. Most Americans would never dream of eating the same dish every day — day after day — for lunch and sometimes dinner. That's left to eccentrics, like Elvis and his peanut butter and banana sandwiches and meatloaf. But on trek, it's best to think of teahouses like a single chain restaurant with a very limited menu. Although many teahouses offer a variety of dishes, only the Nepali staples are consistent in quality and taste: dal bhat, veggie momos, Sherpa stew, veggies and rice, and garlic soup constitute the Fab Five. Any one of these will be great at every teahouse, almost without exception.

We avoided fried foods and meat on the way up, just to err on the side of caution, and chose from the Fab Five. But Dawa made one of them mandatory, requiring that we have at least one bowl of garlic soup every day. "It's an old Sherpa trick," he said. "It thins the blood and helps prevent altitude sickness."

So I resigned myself to having garlic soup for lunch or dinner every day and didn't worry about it. Food was fuel, pure and simple, and I wanted the same fuel the Sherpas used.

After lunch we crossed a suspension bridge and entered another pine forest. Much like the ascent to Namche Bazaar, this trail was steep and dusty, but we were already becoming conditioned, physically and mentally, and with the benefit of our Sherpa fuel, we made the climb in a respectable two hours.

The entrance to Tengboche was at the top of the ridge, and afternoon clouds had descended, drifting around the village rooftops. Dawa, Holly, and I brought up the caboose, as usual, and were five minutes behind the rest of the group. Dawa led us past the famous Tengboche Monastery, across a sloping field, and down to our teahouse, the Tengboche Guest House.

The late afternoon light and clouds gave the village a mysterious feel, heightened by the absence of electricity. Whatever source (hydro, solar, etc.) usually powered the village had gone down several days ago and was not expected to be operational for another month. Even by Nepali standards, we would be roughing it tonight.

A few members of our group were lounging outside on the patio, but most were inside enjoying their afternoon tea. With my

GoPro rolling, I made a high-five circuit through the common room in celebration of another successful day.

We got our room assignments and keys and walked down the darkened hallway. The room was tiny, just large enough to fit two single beds with a space to stand in between. We unloaded our bags and changed into our dry teahouse clothing, hanging our sweaty Merino wool shirts on the curtain rod.

Our evening in Tengboche was low key. After a short walk back to the monastery, which was closed at the time, we had dinner by candlelight and turned in early.

This became the Night of The Pee Bottle. The first three nights on the trek, we had our own private bathrooms, but tonight was going to be different. (Civilized folk don't talk about these things in mixed company, but it is serious business when trekking in Nepal.) At one in the morning, I had two options: 1) Climb out of my toasty sleeping bag into the forty-degree °F air of our room; slip on clothes, shoes, and a headlamp; squeeze out of the doorway partly obstructed by our luggage, and walk down the hallway to a communal toilet. 2) Grab the pee bottle — a plastic, telescoping cylinder that we purchased on Amazon for about three bucks — roll onto my side, and hope for the best.

I chose #2.

I won't lie; it was risky. The cold conditions, the 12,000-foot altitude, and my middle-of-the-night brain made for steep odds. Hanging in the balance was the sanctity of my own sleeping device, the one item that must *not* be compromised during the entirety of the mission. Carefully situating the bottle and my ... *self,* I completed the task with the preciseness of a NASA spaceship docking operation.

Flush with pride at my accomplishment, I snuggled back into my warm and quite dry bag. As I drifted off, a pony whinnied somewhere outside, as if to celebrate my victory.

TEN

NEEDED — ONE HUG FROM A BIG GUY

Knock, knock.

"Namaste! Good morning!"

Hari and Phurba were at our door with tea. I rolled out, careful not to knock over my hero, the pee bottle. I managed to get the door open wide enough to retrieve our cups from the guys after a hearty "Namaste" and "Dhanyabad," which means "Thank you."

I jumped back into my bag.

The steam felt good on my face as I sat up, sipping the hot black tea. A quick peek out the window confirmed another glorious morning, and I had the distinct feeling that we would be greeted with a mountain view that had been hidden by clouds last night.

But first things first. Holly and I would spend the next forty-five minutes bumping into each other as we tried to maneuver in the room to pack our duffels. It was hands down my least favorite part of each day, and I often felt exhausted by the time we got to breakfast.

. . .

I ORDERED OATMEAL WITH RAISINS, DRIZZLING ON A little bit of local honey to satisfy my sweet tooth. As I was finishing, Dawa tapped my shoulder and spoke into my ear.

"Shari got very sick last night," he said. "She's feeling a little better, but she's upset and wants to talk to you. She's outside."

Oh, no! Dread washed over me as I pushed back from the table. I found Shari outside on the patio, seated on the low rock wall. She was in tears as I approached.

"I'm okay, but I just feel really sorry for myself right now," she said with a shaky voice. "Honestly, I just needed a hug from a big guy."

I was happy to give her a shoulder to cry on. Maybe the morale boost could help chase off the nausea.

The rest of the group finished breakfast quickly so we would have time to visit the monastery. We reconvened outside of the teahouse entrance, marveling at the crazy mountains that had unveiled themselves over night. It was astounding, and I hoped the view would help distract Shari from her lingering nausea.

Mornings almost always revealed spectacular views that had been hidden by clouds the prior evening. This was the case in Tengboche. Photo by Bill Shupp.

After a short walk to the monastery, we pulled off our shoes and entered the main room.

With the only light provided by early morning sunshine streaming through the curtained windows, the monastery felt surreal. One solitary monk sat in the middle of the room, chanting a prayer, as we padded around the perimeter. We spoke only in whispers. Once outside, Tenzi explained that the lama who normally blessed the climbers and trekkers was unavailable today, which made me a little uneasy. I hoped it wasn't bad karma.

After purifying our water, filling our reservoirs, and stocking up on snacks, we slid into our backpacks and said goodbye to Teng-boche. As we headed toward the trail, I heard the sounds of youthful voices, and over the top of a nearby grove of trees, a soccer ball appeared before dropping out of sight. There must have been a pitch over there, and kids were already in the midst of a good game.

Amazing, I thought to myself. *People are born here, live a full life, and die having never left these mountains. Who's to say which life is better — theirs or mine?*

The sounds of the game faded as we descended through another thick pine forest. The trail occasionally opened up to reveal spectacular views of both Everest and Ama Dablam, a far more beautiful mountain than its taller and more famous sister.

We stopped for mid-morning tea in Lower Pangboche at Highland Sherpa Resort, an excellent teahouse with a large, comfortable common room. I spent much of this tea stop visiting with Shari. To no one's surprise, she had rebounded considerably and was in relatively good spirits. Shari, Luis, Stefanie, Dawa, and I had tackled the infamous Fiery Gizzard Trail in Middle Tennessee the prior fall, so I knew her to be a tough cookie. She proved me right once again.

Lunch was at Juneli Lodge and Restaurant in the village of Shomare. Upon leaving the cozy teahouse, we realized that the temperatures had dropped significantly. I had started the morning in shirt sleeves, but now it was fleece jacket time. It was also my first opportunity to wear gloves and my reversible Hobnail Trekking knit cap. I was darned proud of that cap.

After a fairly tough ascent on a rocky, narrow section, the trail opened up into a tundra, a wide landscape crisscrossed with thousands of short juniper shrubs and dozens of rutted animal paths. Speaking of animals, we were encountering a lot. By now, the Real McCoy yaks were fairly common, as well as horses, mules, and dzos.

Because we were officially above tree-line now, the scale of the place had moved off the charts, mainly because we could see everything without trees getting in the way. There were also no more windbreaks, so our buffs and knit caps were critical.

This led to lots of jokes about my beard. Freed from several hours of confinement and constant pressure under my buff, my long, wiry whiskers sprang out in random crazy directions, destined to stay that way until I could wet them down with hot water. It was like waking up with bed head. Buff beard became my trademark on the trail and a reliable source of comic relief.

At mid-afternoon we walked into Dingboche, the village that would rank at the top of almost everyone's list by the end of the trip. It was situated in a narrow valley near the foot of Ama Dablam, although we had no idea of that when we walked in. The clouds had descended, the temperature had dropped into the 30s, and we were getting our first taste of snow. Weather notwithstanding, the Hobnail crew was jovial as we walked through the entrance of Peaceful Lodge, probably because Dawa had broken form by setting us up in the first teahouse of the village.

In a warm sunroom, we dropped our packs, slurped our hot teas, and compared war stories of the day's trek. Tenzi also came around and took our dinner orders for later before passing out our room keys. We grabbed our stuff and went searching for our rooms, especially excited because we would be here for two nights.

Holly and I found Room 318 and were dumbfounded when we stepped inside. Wow! It was at least three times larger than our accommodation in Tengboche, had a beautiful set of windows, and twin beds with thick comforters. But the crème de la crème was the bathroom. First of all, it was all ours. Secondly, there was a small vanity and mirror that appeared to be in perfect working order and — wait for it — a very new-looking, western toilet that actually flushed!

I'd never been so excited by a toilet in my life.

After warming up in our bags for a while (Dawa had warned us not to nap during the day), we headed downstairs for another great meal, this time dal bhat for me, roasted potatoes for Holly.

Afterward, Dawa gave us our post-meal briefing regarding tomorrow's schedule and we began our nightly routine, which included having the kitchen staff fill our Nalgene bottles with boiling water. Immediately upon returning to our room, we would slip our bottle into a thermal sock and stuff it into the footbox area of our sleeping bag. We also learned to cram tomorrow's base layers down there, too, as well as laying the next day's pants out under the bag itself. Next morning, warm clothes. Brilliant!

We burrowed down into our respective bags, snug as bugs in rugs.

WE SLEPT LONG AND LUXURIOUSLY IN THIS WONDERFUL lodge, enjoying a 7 a.m. breakfast and re-convening outside in the courtyard at 8. In keeping with tradition, the morning weather was insanely beautiful. Towering above us was the plainly visible summit of Ama Dablam with other peaks all around, each partly obscured halfway up with a lazy cloudbank. It was quiet except for our voices and the pleasant clanking of yak bells from a next-door pasture.

The plan was to ascend nearby Komgamari Ridge to 15,000 feet, hang out for a few minutes, and come back down. Easy, right?

Not so much. The trail was steep and challenging, made even more so by the fact that Dawa started throwing snowballs at me about halfway up. There was just enough snow left over from last night to scrape together a few dirty projectiles. Never one to back down from a snowball fight, I engaged, particularly because I held the high ground, and as Obi-Wan Kenobi taught us in "Star Wars: Episode III—Revenge of the Sith," never attack the person who holds the high ground.

I nailed him twice in the back. Final score: Johnson 2, Sherpa 0.

I would soon regret expending any energy at all on throwing snowballs. At 14,500 feet, gravity seemed intent on pressing my knees and feet down no matter how hard I tried to lift them. This was annoying and I felt angry at gravity. It was walk a little while, rest a little while.

The higher we climbed, the more Dingboche reminded me of a child's play set in the valley below. High above the village, brilliant white clouds swirled about the summit of Ama Dablam. Several times, I stopped just to take in this unimaginable view, trying desperately to commit it to memory, and also because I thought I might puke.

Strangely, the nausea passed and I began feeling stronger as we climbed. Take that, altitude!

I can't claim complete credit for my superhuman resistance to these impressive heights, though, because Holly and I — and most of the group — had been taking Diamox (*Acetazolamide*) since landing in Kathmandu. The drug is widely used in the trekking and mountaineering community as both a preventative of and treatment for acute altitude sickness. According to my crack team of researchers (I looked it up on Wikipedia), Diamox works by decreasing the number of hydrogen ions and bicarbonate in the body.

Since I barely passed chemistry in high school over three decades ago, this means nothing at all to me, though it certainly sounds legit. All I know is that is made my fingertips, toes, and face tingle, somehow shrunk my already small bladder down to little girl-size, and may have kept me from having acute altitude sickness. There's no way to know for sure.

One trekker who shall remain nameless (Rachel) said it made her *butt* tingle.

I was oddly jealous.

Some people like to say that it's somehow "cheating" to take Diamox when climbing and hiking at high altitudes, to which I say, "I'd rather be somehow cheating than somehow dying." It's not like we were taking it to hit more home runs or win more Tour de Frances. (Or would that be Tours de France?)

So complete with tingling fingers and toes, we made it to our destination high above Dingboche, which was like a mini-EBC with a pile of rocks decorated with prayer flags. The entire climb took around three hours, so reaching the top was definitely cause for exploding fist bumps and high fives.

Apparently, cairn-building is a big deal on this mountain, because these carefully balanced mounds of rocks were sticking up all over the place. As a perpetual twelve-year-old boy, I was tempted to knock over some of the bigger ones just for good measure but was afraid I might get beat up, so I fought the urge.

After a short rest and a bunch of photos, we started back down, taking a different route through a yak pasture that led us into the top of the village. This gave us a pleasant, twenty-minute perusal of the entire thing, ending up at Peaceful Lodge where we had started.

The trail back down to Dingboche after our acclimatization hike led through a yak pasture. Photo by Bill Shupp.

That afternoon would be the single longest stretch of free time we would get during our trekking days. We enjoyed a leisurely lunch of the normal fare and arranged to meet in the courtyard at around 2:30 p.m. to walk to a nearby bakery for a 3 o'clock showing of the movie "Everest." This sounded like great fun, watching people suffer tragic and painful deaths in the cold conditions and high altitude of the Himalayas — exactly where we happened to be at the moment. It would be like watching "Jaws" immediately before slathering yourself with SPAM and taking a late-night ocean dip off Amity Island.

But it wasn't to be. We arrived at the bakery to find the place at full capacity, packed with other masochistic hikers and climbers. Oh, well. We hoofed it back to the Peaceful Lodge and spent the afternoon doing our own things.

To no one's surprise, Holly took a nap in defiance of Dawa's no-napping instructions. Since her natural sleep pattern is roughly akin to that of a fourteen-year-old house cat, I wasn't too worried, though annoyed.

Before splitting up, several of us decided to meet back in the sunroom before dinner for a Mike Maxim salsa lesson.

That's right — salsa at 14,000 feet.

THE LESSON STARTED PROMPTLY AT 6 P.M., WITH ALL BUT three of us along with all the Sherpas. The plan was to master a simple salsa routine to be filmed at Base Camp, making us all instant YouTube sensations.

After we moved the table and chairs out of the way, Mike lined us up in rows, five across and three deep, facing in one direction with him at the front of the room. He showed us a few of the basic steps in salsa dancing. After each demonstration, he would say things like "See how easy this is? Nothing to it! You can do this!"

I heard those words in my brain, but my feet heard "See how hard this is? It's impossible! You can't do it and, oh, by the way, you look like a buffoon."

To make matters worse, Mike announced that we would be dancing with each other. The ladies would rotate around the room, partnering with each guy for a few minutes until Mike yelled, "Change partner!" I pitied each poor woman when they got around to me. For them, it was like trying to dance with a 6'5" deck chair in a high wind.

"Oh, you're good!" they would say to me through a ghastly smile of clenched teeth, inwardly pleading for Mike to call for a partner change.

At one point, I glanced out the window and made eye contact with a yak that was standing in the blowing snow, chewing his cud and staring at me. Lucky yak.

Ever the optimist, Mike soldiered on and, by the end of the hour, had us actually dancing a "routine" of sorts as we strained to hear the salsa music from his cell phone.

The funny thing, though, was that although none of the trekkers were very gifted as dancers, we had seen enough salsa dancing in popular culture to *kind of* know what it's supposed to look like. Dawa, who had experienced only two immersive years of American culture, was actually pretty good.

But the other Sherpas, particularly Tenzi, were train wrecks. Having never seen someone salsa dancing, they had to start entirely from scratch. So in typical, optimistic, Sherpa fashion, they just went for it and did their own thing, smiling and laughing the entire time. Tenzi essentially spun around in circles like a laughing whirling dervish.

Remember, this was partner dancing, which made Tenzi challenging for the ladies. I was almost good by comparison.

Almost.

I couldn't imagine that other trekking groups were having near as much fun as we were, and I couldn't have been more proud of our team. It was clear, though, that none of us would soon be invited onto "Dancing with the Stars." (Except for Mike, who actually *was* invited onto DWTS.)

Mercifully, it ended and we went to dinner. Later, I wrote up my trip notes quickly and bee-lined for my sleeping bag, exhausted but happy.

It had been a great day of bonding and shared experience. I made a mental note to include "Salsa Lessons at 14K feet" as part of our future trek offerings. Now, if I could only get Mike to go on every trek. . . .

ELEVEN

A BITTER PILL

L ike the previous night, I slept well despite a bevy of crazy dreams, including one that had Hari and Phurba delivering our morning tea dressed like Carnivale dancers and doing salsa moves. When the actual good morning knock came, I opened the door suspiciously and peered out.

"Namaste!" they said in unison, dressed quite normally.

Oh, thank God. I gratefully took our teas and retreated to the warmth of my sleeping bag.

As we were heading into the dining room some forty-five minutes later, Jeff called my name and waved me over. I could tell by the look on his face that something was wrong. Since our first night in Phakding, he had been battling sleep apnea, and I don't think he had been winning.

"I think I might have to call it," he said to me quietly. "Last night was more of the same. I literally couldn't sleep at all and I'm concerned that it will get worse as we get higher." Even though sleep deprivation would undo anybody in this situation, Jeff was most concerned with falling asleep and possibly suffocating before he could wake himself up. He was afraid that there was simply not enough oxygen and air pressure at this altitude to keep his airways open.

After consulting with both Shari and Rachel, he made his decision. He would announce it after breakfast.

In just seven days, Jeff had become a beloved team member. His laconic, deadpan humor, his wealth of outdoor knowledge, and his genuine concern for others made him irreplaceable.

After a meal of hard-boiled eggs and Tibetan bread, we packed up and met in the courtyard, where Natalie led our morning prayer and we grabbed a group photo. Then Jeff asked to address the group.

"Guys, I hate to tell you this, but I've decided not to go on," he said. "I just feel like it's irresponsible to put myself at risk and possibly create a bad situation for you guys. It's been a terrible decision to make and I know it's going to haunt me, but I think it's for the best. Dawa has already called the helicopter."

Stunned silence. This was monumental. After months of planning and training, not to mention all the years of outdoor experiences, to be undone by sleep apnea was unthinkable. This was a man who was used to routinely setting, training for, and ultimately reaching his goals. We were all in tears, and Jeff was struggling to hold it together.

As everyone walked up to hug the Oregonian, I hung back to let each group member say their goodbye, then gave my old friend a tight embrace.

"You're going to come back with Nick and get this thing done," I told him. "We will figure this out."

Jeff nodded, emotional. "I'm not going to watch y'all hike away," he said. "Can't do that." He turned and walked back toward the Peaceful Lodge entrance.

The group was silent as we ascended the ridge. Later, we heard a helicopter echoing up the valley and wondered if it was his.

. . .

At some point in the morning, the trail split like it had done above Namche Bazaar, with the acclimatization hikers continuing up and those bound for Lobuche breaking off and heading up the valley. It felt a little sad to leave the comfort and safety of Dingboche. We all knew that from here on out, the creature comforts were essentially over.

As we topped a wide slope, the vista before us revealed our task: we would be walking along a gently rising ridge situated adjacent to a massif of snowy peaks with a valley in between. The ground was a tundra covered in a lichen-ish vegetation that was more of a skin for the soil than anything else. It was mottled and gray, so Holly and I called it "elephant skin." Here and there, small groupings of juniper bushes and boulders jutted out of the ground.

This walk was one of the most enjoyable yet, and not particularly taxing. We moved along in conversational groups, duos, or singles depending on how the mood was striking us. But although this hike wasn't difficult, we also didn't seem to be getting anywhere. Ever the philosopher, I've come up with a couple reasons why.

First, although we were probably walking at the same rate of speed as earlier in the trek, the landscape here was much more open and expansive. Imagine yourself driving 55 on a narrow, two-lane country road. Seems fast, right? Now do 55 on a six-lane interstate. Seems like you're barely moving. It's all a matter of perception.

Secondly, the scale of the Himalayas is unlike what most people have ever experienced.

Everything is huge.

The section of trail between Dingboche and the tiny village of Thukla is awe-inspiring. Photo by Bill Shupp.

So if you see an object in the distance — let's say a house — that in Tennessee should take about ten minutes to reach by foot, you can bet it's an hour's hike in the Himalayas. Our perception of distance is thrown out of whack by the sheer size of the surrounding mountains. Conversely, a native Sherpa would probably be surprised by how close objects are upon first visiting other, less mountainous areas of the world.

We continued moving along the elephant skin, wondering if we would ever reach our destination. Mid-morning, we came upon a couple of stone huts with dry-stack rock walls enclosing a small pasture—yak keeper cottages. The backs of the structures were built into a berm in the ridge and the roofs were thin slabs of slate, framed by the towering mountains behind them. We spent some time here taking photos and videos, some of which would prove to be my favorites.

Eventually, the wide trail narrowed and became rockier. We curved right and were greeted around the bend by the astonishing site of the Khumbu Glacier's endpoint high above us, a gigantic pile of rubble. Below the glacier was a steep jumble of boulders and meltwater that constituted the headwaters of the Dudh Kosi River. For nearly an hour we picked our way carefully through this streamed of boulders and crystal-clear water to our lunch destination on the other side, a tiny village called Thukla, Dughla, or Cincinnati, depending on whom you asked. Again, due to the skewed scale, it never seemed to be getting any closer. I felt like an ant trying to cross a football field.

Eventually, our diligence paid off and we reached our rest area along the EBC interstate. We climbed a steep embankment into the village, basically a clearing upon which a single teahouse and a couple other structures were built at the base of an imposing hillside leading up to the glacier. I could see the trail threading up through the boulders and switchbacks, and made a mental note to eat plenty of lunch.

I was going to need it.

Just to make things more fun, clouds were rolling in and tiny snow pebbles were beginning to pelt us.

The teahouse was crowded with trekkers, but Dawa had called ahead and reserved our table space. Soon we were seated and sipping on delicious hot teas. The Sherpa stew that Holly and I ordered was equally good, and we made a point to eat everything even though our appetites were beginning to wane a little, a common issue at altitude.

Toward the end of lunch, Luis said, "Uh, oh" and pointed out the window.

It was snowing in earnest, now.

We looked at each other and shrugged. These were the cards we were dealt, and we knew the weather would eventually take issue with our leisurely trek. Now it was calling our hand.

LUNCH NOW FINISHED, WE SPENT SEVERAL MINUTES extracting down jackets, rain shells, and gloves from our packs. Sufficiently bundled, we left the relative security of the teahouse, stopping to pet a very enthusiastic, fluffy puppy on the way.

The ascent above Thukla was a beast. Narrow, rocky, and steep, it gave us a nice precursor to what we would face tomorrow on the way to Base Camp. We climbed steadily for nearly an hour as snow swirled and the temperatures continued to drop.

About halfway up, we passed a trekker on his way down.

"I hope you guys like snow," he said with a German accent, laughing.

Oh, boy.

Suddenly, we were at the top, a large plateau called Chukpa Lare, the Pass of Monuments. My altitude app read 15,750 feet. Through the blowing snow and fog I could see dozens of stone and cement monuments erected to honor those who had lost their lives on Everest. Some had photos of the climbers and informational placards attached. Others were draped in faded prayer flags or adorned with heaps of pebbles at their base.

We spent several minutes at the large stone monument for American guide Scott Fischer, whose death was made famous in Jon Krakauer's book *Into Thin Air* and the movie "Everest."

In these dreamlike conditions, the entire place was surreal and slightly creepy.

The memorials at Chukpa Lare were both poignant and a little creepy in the deep fog and snow. Photo by Bill Shupp.

Although I made a conscious effort not to think too much

about it, the concept of dying in this remote place did occasionally cross my mind, and Chukpa Lare was a grim reminder not to take life for granted. On the flip side, though, it gave me a burst of adrenaline to know that our trekkers were pushing themselves beyond the norm and into a place most people will never experience because it's so far outside their comfort zone. Sometimes a modicum of danger and mortality is necessary for an adventure that makes the most of our human condition.

Enough about death already—it was life I was after, and I was determined to escape the negative energy and conquer this long-standing goal. Time to move past the monuments!

(Honestly, I wanted to leave because my pinky toes were getting a little cold from standing, and I hate it when my pinky toes get cold.)

In contrast to some of the ascents we'd faced, the trail between the memorials and Lobuche was fairly level and easy. Nonetheless, Holly's knees continued to bother her so we took it slow. Hari stayed with us while the rest of the group moved ahead.

We were ascending a fairly sizable hill, huffing and puffing, when I became aware that a small group was passing us on the left, moving quickly. First came a Sherpa guide, then a trekker, then a porter. They passed us like we were standing still.

But it was the trekker who made this moment so memorable. First I noticed that he was older than I, which was annoying. Then I saw that he was wearing a short-sleeved plaid shirt and a ball cap, which was just plain crazy. Then I realized that he was flying over the tundra on *two prosthetic legs*. I couldn't help but stare, not because of his legs, but because of how flippin' fast he was moving on them.

When he got far enough away, Hari turned to me.

"That was Mark Inglis, the famous mountaineer," he said. "He's the first double-amputee to summit Everest."

Well, that explains it, I thought. *As a mere mortal Doofus Dad, I'm still pretty proud of myself.*

. . .

As we topped a ridge in late afternoon, Lobuche appeared in a shallow valley. It was a collection of around ten teahouses and a few varied outbuildings that looked like they'd been plopped down in the middle of an earth-moving or strip-mining operation. All around were naturally-occurring piles of dirt and boulders, no doubt scooped up and deposited there eons ago by the Khumbu Glacier or some version of it. Were it not for the buildings and the snowcapped peaks, I could have sworn we'd landed on the moon.

As we walked into our teahouse, oddly named Himalayan Chain Resort Eco-Lodge, I had my first altitude-related headache. After drinking about half a liter of water and a hot lemon tea, it went away.

As we expected, the rooms were super basic, divided by a thin piece of plywood. Holly and I had begun our normal routine of situating our sleeping bags and the supplied blanket or comforter, me in the left bed, her in the right, she suddenly exclaimed "YUCK!"

I looked over and there, in the middle of the bed, clearly visible on the fitted sheet, plain as the nose on your face was a . . . wait for it. . . POOP stain.

We just stood there, staring.

"Um, what the hell do I do about this?" Holly finally asked, her eyes affixed on the repugnant smudge. "Homie ain't sleepin' on that."

"Even with your sleeping bag on top?" I ventured. "Maybe that's not even what it is. You should smell it."

I regretted the words immediately.

"Oh, HEY-UL no!" Holly fairly shouted. "Are you kidding me??"

"OK, just sit tight and let me go see if they can replace that sheet," I said, afraid she would make us change beds and completely wreck the feng shui we had developed over the past week. Plus, I didn't want to sleep on it either. "Just sit on my bed for a minute."

I trotted down to the common room and found Dawa enjoying a well-deserved cup of tea. I pulled him aside.

"Hey man, red alert," I hissed. "The sheet on Holly's bed has a poop stain."

"Really?? A poop stain?"

"Yep. Poop stain. What can we do?" It's not like we were at Embassy Suites.

Dawa pursed his brow in concentration. "OK, go back to your room," he said. "I'll think of something."

I trotted back through the darkened hallway to room 104. Holly and I sat side by side on my bed, staring at the poop stain as if it might suddenly squeal and scamper across the room like a scene from "Alien."

Soon there was a knock on the door and Tenzi entered. He pulled off the offending sheet, disappeared into the hallway, and returned with a curtain. He quickly spread the lovely floral pattern across the bed.

"Sorry!" he said with concern. "This will have to do for now."

So that night, Holly slept in a sleeping bag, on a curtain, on a bed at 16,207 feet. Thus ended The Great Poop Stain Incident of 2018 and Day 7 of our trek.

TWELVE

TO THE ROOFTOP OF THE WORLD — BIG E

Wake up was at 4:30 a.m. Even though I expected it, I was still slightly annoyed by the chipperness of Hari and Phurba when they knocked with our wake-up tea.

"Namaste! Good morning!" they said in unison with giant toothy grins.

Yeah, yeah, whatever. Just give me the damn tea.

Oh, of course I didn't say that. But I thought it.

Holly woke up on her curtain bed feeling terrible. She had a substantial headache and was dealing with waves of nausea, but thanks to her longstanding No-Vomiting policy, it never progressed.

(Note: In the twenty-one years we've been married, I can only remember one time, maybe twice, that Holly vomited. She so despises it that she has written up a strict contract with her digestive system to always bypass vomiting as an option.)

We quickly took our morning Diamox and O2 Gold pills and drank a bunch of water, which made her feel somewhat better. She also took some Tylenol as directed by Dawa.

Even with her physical challenges, Holly was upbeat because, after purchasing a WiFi card last night, we had been able to text with our 10-year-old, Pete, for the first time. It was a gigantic relief for both of us.

It was also easily the shortest text exchange we've ever had with our loquacious 10-year-old, thanks to the spotty WiFi. But it was enough.

By the time we got our stuff packed and down to the dining room, most of the group was finishing their breakfast. It was worked out that Holly, myself, Tenzi, Hari, and Gina would leave around twenty minutes behind the main group. Gina was battling a persistent bout of dysentery, although from her always-buoyant attitude, you'd never know it.

The sun was just topping the mountains as we stepped outside, revealing an astounding site: it had snowed about two inches during the night, just enough to cover everything. Not only that, but the soaring mountains surrounding us were now plainly visible. Wispy clouds streaked across a deep azure sky.

My first reaction to this was excitement because I love hiking through snow as long as I have the proper gear, which I did. But my second, more powerful thought was, *Oh, crap. The footing will be treacherous for Holly's knees.*

But there was no debate that the environment in which we found ourselves was otherworldly.

It would be a long day — one of the longest — so we paced ourselves and walked slowly, hoping to catch the yeti. The footing was indeed slippery, but we took our time. As the morning progressed, we began encountering more and more trekkers, and sometimes the narrow trail became log-jammed with both people and pack animals.

One of the strange things about this day was something that I've heard other people who have done this trek express: they weren't able to remember a lot of it. At first, I thought this was only me, and that maybe my fifteen years as a long-haired, folk-rock road musician were coming home to roost. (You can make your own inferences about that.) But others I've since talked with have had the same experience.

Did that actually happen? Did I just dream that?

As you may have guessed, having read this far, I have a couple theories about this.

Altitude. Something about spending time above 16K feet messes with your memory. Seriously.

More likely, though, I think that we just aren't able to fully process and store memories that are unusually exciting, stressful, or removed from our normal sphere of experience. It's like when people say they can't remember their wedding day very well.

I'm guessing it's a little of both. But the honest truth is that I've had to refer to video and notes that I took during the trip to remember certain parts of it clearly. Otherwise, it's a hazy dream.

The Hobnail team was part of a long string of trekkers advancing through the snow toward Gorak Shep and Everest Base Camp. Photo by Mike Maxim.

By the time we arrived at the Buddha Lodge in Gorak Shep, the last village before EBC, most of the snow had either melted or evaporated. (I was never sure about this. It just seemed to disappear.) It had taken around four hours to arrive, so we were happy to unload and have lunch. (I have no memory of what I ate.)

Afterward, Dawa instructed us to remove all unnecessary gear from our packs and only bring just enough water. We would leave our stuff in our rooms and travel as light as possible to EBC.

The first leg of the hike began deceptively easy and level. We started by passing the iconic yellow-and-red "This way to Everest Base Camp" sign, with several members of the group having their photos taken with it. After about a half mile, though, the joke was over. The trail became an up-and-down affair comprising wobbly stones and boulders, yak trains and porters, and either faster trekkers or people walking in the opposite direction. Every time we topped a hill, we could plainly see the yellow tents of Base Camp, but — what with the strange problems with scale and perception — we never seemed to get any closer.

A couple hours in, Holly stopped in front of me.

"I just don't think I can walk another step," she said, her voice thick with emotion. "My knees have had it."

I put an arm around her.

"It's a WOD, honey," I said, referring to our ever-present Crossfit motivator. "It's a long WOD, but you can and will do it. This is what we've been working for over the past two years and it's almost here."

She sighed and wiped a couple tears.

"Okay. Let's go."

An hour later, we were close. Clouds, unfortunately, had settled down low, but we could still clearly see the infamous Khumbu Icefall at the head of the glacier and the foot of the Western ridge of Everest. Like marching ants, several hundred trekkers were picking their way through the boulder fields and across piles of slippery scree to and from the prayer-flag-decorated stones that constitute EBC. As we approached, we passed a group of Sherpas who appeared to be digging out a new section of trail. I had the impression that it wasn't a planned thing, but a decision that had been made on the fly.

As I passed, I made a mental note that it wouldn't take long at the rate they were moving, which was remarkable.

In a final cruel twist, the trail plunged precipitously downhill through a steep and fairly dangerous boulder field onto the glacier itself, and then up again, throwing another challenge at Holly's beleaguered knees. As we struggled up the final ascent, a thick sheet of falling snow rushed at us, as if heralding our impending victory. We approached the EBC pile of rocks to whoops and yells from our other group members who had been waiting for us.

Hari and Dawa approached Holly, embracing her, and she dissolved into tears. Then, Phurba and Dawa — more tears. Eventually, she found me in the crowd and buried her face in my down-jacket chest.

"You did it, honey," I whispered as she hid her face. "You made it."

It was a nice little exchange.

MORE TEAM MEMBERS CAME OVER TO CONGRATULATE Holly, and I had a couple things I needed to do, so I walked off a short distance to drop my pack. As I did, Mark Inglis, the double-amputee, walked into camp next to me. I approached him, shaking his hand and congratulating him on his accomplishments.

All around us, the celebration had begun in earnest, and for the next ten minutes we embraced each other, exchanged high fives and fist bumps, and took copious selfies.

"Mark! Over here!"

Dawa waved me over to where he and the other Sherpas were standing and handed me a shot glass filled with clear liquor.

"This is how we celebrate a successful trek!" he said. "You are part of my team."

I couldn't have been more proud or moved, and we downed our shots together. (Whatever it was, it was excellent and warmed me up nicely.)

Dawa then gathered us all together for a group shot with our Hobnail Trekking Co. flag. Bill Shupp, our trekker/photographer, set up the shot with his camera on a tripod, tripped the timer, and then ran to get in the picture.

Snap!

We all cheered in unison. It was simply a wonderful moment, one of the best.

Our group was ecstatic about reaching Everest Base Camp despite the heavy, blowing snow and 17-degree temperature. Photo by Bill Shupp.

As I walked back to my backpack, a couple of young American guys asked if I would take their photo in front of the stones.

"Sure!" I said. "Y'all ready?"

"Give us one second," one of them replied.

Then to the astonishment of myself and everybody standing around, these guys removed their down jackets and stripped off top layers until they were bare-chested. With the snow creating near whiteout conditions and the temperature hovering at 17 degrees °F, I photographed these crazy dudes at Everest Base Camp, their chests thrust forward in defiance of Mother Nature. After I snapped the shutter release of their camera, another raucous cheer went up among the onlookers.

It was Mardi Gras at the top of the world.

DAWA'S VOICE CUT THROUGH THE DIN.

"Okay! Let's get ready to head back!"

Our group immediately began readying themselves for the return trip. My GoPro would later show that Holly and I were in Base Camp for a total of seventeen minutes.

As I slid back into my pack, Holly spoke quietly into my ear.

"I don't know if I can make it back," she said. "I'm just spent."

I gave her a tight squeeze.

"You can and you will," I said. "You know why?"

"Why?"

"Because you have no choice."

She nodded and put her game face on.

(Note: It was two days later when somebody offhandedly mentioned that we had forgotten our salsa routine at Base Camp. None of us thought of it. No YouTube fame for us!)

We started out in front this time, with Hari leading the way. To our astonishment, Hari detoured onto the new section of trail that was built not thirty minutes ago, effectively cutting off the steep boulder field I mentioned earlier. I'd even hazard to say that we were the first Western trekkers to use it, and we were grateful we didn't have to ascend the boulder field.

The trek back was slow and deliberate, every step carefully placed. I worried about Holly the entire way, but she had switched into Stubborn Mode, which meant she would make it come hell or high water.

Around ninety minutes in, we turned a corner and were greeted by a most welcome site — our yak man, Ngwang, holding tin cups and a large Thermos.

"Namaste!" he shouted. "Congratulations!"

We dropped our packs and found flat rocks for seats, and Ngwang poured us full cups of hot mango juice.

Like Popeye with his spinach, I could feel the strength returning to my limbs as the steaming manna warmed my core. Fueled by mango and flush with the glow of accomplishment, we finished the last hour of the hike, headed straight for our room, and crawled into our sleeping bags for a non-sanctioned nap, careful not to tell Dawa later.

That night at dinner, I can't recall a lot of conversation. I think the squad was whipped, both physically and emotionally. We were struggling to eat half the food of which, just a couple days ago, we were begging for seconds.

But we were happy nonetheless. We had met our goal.

It was an incredible feeling of accomplishment, even better than that time I fixed the bathroom faucet by myself after watching an instructional video. And that was pretty good!

Only one obstacle left before we head down, I thought to myself later as I drifted off to sleep in my bag. *Kalapathar.*

I WAS ALREADY AWAKE WHEN PHURBA TAPPED ON OUR door at 4:10 a.m. It had been a fitful night of sleep, full of weird dreams and on-and-off wakefulness. We were sleeping side-by-side on a double bed, and I had to crawl over Holly's legs to get out, fumbling in the 25-degree darkness. Today was her birthday, so I had to resist the urge to break into song.

That would come later.

"Namaste and good morning," Phurba whispered at the door. "Let's meet in the dining room in fifteen minutes."

I quickly dressed, trying not to make noise. Of our group of fifteen, only three of us would be making the optional climb up Kalapathar this morning due to the challenges of the previous day, so I didn't want to disturb the folks who opted out.

The more I woke up, the more I realized how lousy I felt. My head was pounding and a touch of nausea was swimming around in my stomach. I hoped my morning tea and a healthy dose of water would do the trick.

Phurba and Dawa were waiting for me in the dining room.

"Mike and Bill have already left," Dawa said, handing me a cup of black tea. "So it will just be us this morning."

The tea and water helped my headache and stomach a little, but I was certainly not at 100 percent. But as the owner and ceremonial leader of the trip, bailing on this morning's hike didn't seem like a viable option.

We left the teahouse and threaded our way down a series of icy stone staircases through the darkened village, our headlamps illuminated our steps through heavy, blowing snow. Even walking through Gorak Shep, I was having a hard time keeping up with the two Sherpas.

From the bottom of the last set of steps, a path led across a level, flat area to the base of the dark, conical mountain. From a distance, the trail up Kalapathar seemed fairly gentle, but up close it was a different story. There was no gradual climb; it went from totally flat to very steep in the course of two feet, as if the mountain was a giant cone that someone had plopped down on a table top. Very weird, indeed.

My vision is notoriously bad in poor light, and it felt as though I was walking through a dream. No matter how high the intensity of my headlamp beam, I just couldn't see clearly in the blowing snow. It created an eerie, out-of-body sensation that made me question whether or not I was actually awake.

I plodded up the steep incline trying to match Dawa's pace, which was already much slower than normal. Pretty soon, we were higher than the EBC altitude, a fact confirmed not only by my iPhone altimeter but my lungs as well. For the past two years, I had been wondering how altitude would affect my performance, and now I knew. Even after days of acclimatization, each step became a chore and I had to pause and rest after every fifteen feet or so.

After a while, the winds quieted down to nothing and the snow stopped falling. Without the wind in my ears, I was more aware of the sounds of my own huffing and puffing.

Slowly . . . catches . . . Yeti, I wheezed to myself. Glancing back at the darkened village below, I envisioned the other members of the team snug in their bags, snoring and dreaming of steaming plates of fish and rice being served to them by lovely Stepford Wives flight attendants smiling demurely.

I plodded on.

At around 5:45, I noticed the sky had turned from black to a deep blue, and I could just make out the summit of Everest, a plume of snow hanging still against a smattering of stars. We were halfway up a long, gentle slope that ended in a final steep ascent. I could see a few bobbing headlamps above me near what I perceived as Kalapathar's summit, and I wondered if they belonged to Mike and Bill.

After another ten steps, a feeling of completion struck me. I knew I was done.

"I think I'm good right here," I called out to Dawa. To my surprise, he seemed absolutely fine with that.

"Yes, the view from here is just as good," he said, walking back to where I was standing. "Let's just hang out here for a while."

Dawa, Phurba, and I found comfortable rocks and sat down,

enjoying our ringside seat to the day breaking around us. After several minutes, my breathing returned to normal and I actually felt good.

We shot several photos and videos from our vantage point as a few other trekkers plodded past us. I was secretly pleased to see that many had stopped much lower down.

From the summit of Kalapathar, Bill Shupp made this stunning image of the sun breaking over Mount Everest.

And then, it got cold.

Our lack of movement and exposure to the elements was catching up with us, and I began feeling it in my toes. I got up and began walking in circles, climbing a few feet and then returning to the starting point in an attempt to warm up, but I could see that nothing short of actually increasing my heart rate would have much effect.

The sky had now lightened significantly behind Big E, so I shot several more photos and walked over to Dawa.

"What do you think? I'm satisfied if you are."

"Yep, I'm good. Let's get Phurba and get the heck out of here."

Music to my ears. We headed down quickly, nearly trotting. What had taken ninety minutes to climb took about fifteen minutes to descend. Soon, we were in the lodge dining room, huddled around the yak-dung-fueled stove with a cup of hot tea in our hands.

In retrospect, I do have regrets about not going to the top of Kalapathar, but it's easy to second-guess myself in the 70-degree comfort of my Tennessee living room, feet propped up with a cat on my lap. In the moment, however, stopping was probably the right decision to make. My EBC trek topped out at 17,800 feet, and I was darn proud of it. That's more than 3,000 feet higher than the highest point in the continental United States.

Cool.

THIRTEEN
HOLLY'S KNEES AND THE YETI'S LAIR

I had been sitting at the stove for about twenty minutes when Rachel appeared in the still mostly empty room. She told me that Holly was awake, felt terrible, and was asking for me. I hoofed it down two flights of stairs to our room.

Holly, still buried in her sleeping bag, was moaning.

"I feel like total crap," she rasped, barely audible. "My head hurts, my knees ache, and I'm nauseous. To make matters worse, I got up in the middle of the night and tried to use the pee bottle with my she-nis and peed all over the floor and myself."

A little background is required here. Before the trip, Holly purchased one of those little rubber devices that allows a woman to urinate standing up. I forget what the name brand was, but Holly immediately began calling it her "she-nis," which I thought was quite clever and rather hilarious.

"Oh, geez," I said. "What can I do to help you?"

"Probably nothing," she croaked. "I just need to get to a lower altitude."

"Well, let's get you up then. The sooner we get some food and water into you, the better."

By the time we got packed and upstairs to the dining room, the rest of the group was finishing breakfast. As happened the day before, Tenzi and Hari stayed back with us while the others started out on what would be a very long day of trekking.

It took about three hours to hike from Gorak Shep back down to Lobuche, and the going was slow. Since vomiting was off the table for Holly, she dealt with the nausea in other ways and drank extra water at Tenzi's request. The good news was that the weather cooperated and the morning was in its usual fine form, allowing us to strip off our down jackets in favor of our mid-layer fleece.

As we approached Lobuche just before noon, Holly came to a halt.

"Honey, my knees are killing me," she said in a whimper. "I just don't know if I can go on."

We were within minutes of the lodge, which was in plain view.

"Come on," I said. "Just take it slow. Let's get in where we can sit down and give you a break."

After a few moments, she awkwardly limped into the teahouse, just as our group was leaving for the next leg of the day's trek. Rachel gave Holly a large dose of Tylenol, which seemed to help. By the time we have finished our lunches, her knee felt remarkably better.

BY EARLY AFTERNOON WE HAD REACHED CHUKPA LARE, the Pass of Monuments. It seemed much less ominous in bright sunshine, so we hung out for a few minutes. Then it was time to tackle the rocky descent to tiny Thukla. As we gingerly picked our way down through the boulders, I happened to look to my left at a mountainside that was adjacent to us. (If this mountain had a name, I never knew it.) Something caught my eye.

About halfway up this mountain, there appeared to be an out-of-place structure. Embedded into a huge, gray formation of stone was what resembled a set of enormous wooden doors, like something Frodo and Samwise would've been forced to enter at the risk of encountering an army of bloodthirsty orcs. I stopped in my tracks and stared.

Looking closer, there seemed to be a black humanoid figure standing by the door.

What the hell…?

Had I stumbled across the yeti's lair??

"Tenzi, what the heck is that?" I said, pointing out the structure.

"I don't know!" he said, frowning. "I've never noticed that."

I grabbed my iPhone, zoomed into the mountain, and snapped a picture. Later, as we had tea at Thukla, I reviewed the picture with Russ, who was wildly excited by my description. On closer inspection, it was probably an odd, square stone with a splash of black coloration that resembled a large man.

But maybe it wasn't. You decide.

Yeti's lair or weird rock formation? I'm not sure. I'm going with Yeti's lair. Or perhaps the Grinch's house. See the black figure standing at the right?

Holly's knees were holding up for now. By some miracle, the episode she had at Lobuche seemed to correct itself and she was getting by.

After leaving Thukla, we took a different route through the boulder field/river bed than we'd taken two days ago. This trail led us down into the Pheriche Valley. Once there, we were essentially walking on level ground. We had dropped altitude dramatically, and I could almost feel the increased density of oxygen as I breathed in the mountain air.

Maybe because we all felt more oxygenated, our little group was in high spirits. We chatted with Tenzi and Hari about their families, where they were raised, and what they wanted out of life. We told them about ourselves and our backgrounds. Tenzi's distinctive laugh reverberated through the valley when I described how I had traveled the country living the rock-star life (minus the fame, riches, and consistent three meals a day).

Actually, he laughed a little *too* hard at this. I snorted and pulled my cap further down over my bald head, adjusting the waist strap of my backpack over my 52-year-old, non-rock-star paunch. My crazy, snow-white, Santa Claus-like, buff-beard swayed in the breeze.

Why is all this so hard to believe?!

Annoyed, I changed the subject.

A cold steady wind swept through the long, half-pipe-shaped valley. On our left was the ridge we had traversed two days ago when we encountered the yak-man shacks and elephant-skin ground. On our right, several enormous peaks jutted into the clouds, their sides streaked with rockslides, mini-glaciers, and frozen waterfalls. The head of the valley was clogged with a much larger glacier, as wide as the Khumbu. The lower end, where we were headed, intersected a larger valley through which the Imja Khola flowed, fed in part by the melt-water stream we were trekking alongside. Also at the lower end, Ama Dablam towered, overlooking the entire region like a massive lighthouse.

We passed through a small gathering of yak-keeper cottages that were currently occupied. Tenzi approached one keeper to ask if we could look inside his home but was waved off. This was the one time during the trip that a local reacted negatively to our presence. I didn't take it personally. He was probably just having a bad morning.

In the distance, we could clearly see our destination — Pheriche. It seemed that we could reach out and touch it, but again, the enormity of the mountains beside us threw off our depth perception and the trek took much longer than I thought it should have. But I enjoyed it immensely and gave thanks for the level, relatively gentle trail, knowing that this was a Godsend for Holly's beleaguered knees. A sense of dread had been creeping into my brain ever since Base Camp and then intensifying since Lobuche. It nagged at me constantly.. *Can she actually make it back to Lukla?*

I had my doubts.

"WELL THE LEFT FOOT, IT'LL FOLLOW / WHERE THE RIGHT FOOT HAS *traveled*"

The Jimmy Buffett lyric stuck in my head, incongruous yet appropriate. If nothing else, hiking teaches you to keep that right foot moving and, regardless of fatigue, you'll soon find yourself in a different, sometimes wonderful, location. Mobility is an amazing gift.

In spite of the discrepancies in scale, we actually did walk into Pheriche pretty much on time. It was a neat, efficient little village built around the Himalayan Rescue Association outpost, a small hospital and the first stop for injured or sick climbers and trekkers who need to be stabilized before transfer to Kathmandu. After checking out the strange, stainless-steel monument to fallen climbers located outside the front door of the hospital, we found our way to our teahouse for the night, the Pheriche Resort.

Although "resort" was a bit of a stretch, the place was clean and comfortable except that the structure was clearly built for hobbits. If I was standing, I was usually hunkering to avoid clocking my head on the ceiling or smashing a light bulb.

The rest of the gang was enjoying their teas when we arrived, and cheers went up. After we visited for a while, Shari whispered to me that the group had something in store for Holly's birthday at dinner, and to show up a few minutes late.

No problem. We got to our room and went straight for the sleeping bags. I knew my wife would immediately drift off, so I stayed awake, watching a movie on my iPad until just the right time, and then woke her up.

"Let's go, Sweetie," I called to her. "We're almost late for dinner."

We shuffled through the now-darkened hallway — me, the Hunchback of Notre Dame and her, a battered soldier — and into the dining room.

Immediately a blaring chorus of noisemakers honked in unison. Not only our group but everyone in the room was armed with the party props and nobody was afraid to use them. The din was nearly deafening.

"SURPRISE!!" they all shouted.

Exhausted, in pain, and now suffering from a nasty head cold, Holly could only attempt a smile, her face contorting into an emotional grimace, tears welling in her eyes. I led her to her seat of honor as Shari placed a conical party hat over her wool beanie.

One by one, each team member came and gave Holly a much-needed hug. Phurba and Ngwang placed multiple ceremonial scarves over her neck and bowed to acknowledge her birthday.

Holly was then presented with a bag of gifts: an authentic Nepalese beanie, a pair of funny socks, a couple of candy suckers, and a real yak bell. Just when we thought the fun was over, the lights blinked and went out. Tenzi walked into the room with an enormous, flat apple pie into which was jabbed several lit birthday candles. "Happy Birthday" was scrawled in sugar sprinkled around the pie. After they all serenaded us, everyone got a small piece of pie, Sherpas included.

We returned to the room that night sick and exhausted, but happy.

SOMETIME IN THE MIDDLE OF THE NIGHT, MY LOVELY dream of sitting under the Caribbean sun on a St. Croix beach, feet in the water and my toes being nibbled at by a school of minnows — all while being served margaritas by matching China Southern flight attendants — was rudely interrupted by a banging on our wall.

"Hey, guys!" It was Steve Tudor's voice coming through the thin plywood beside Holly. "We're locked in our room! Can you open our door?"

"What?"

"We're locked in our room! We can't get out! Can you open the door?!"

After taking a second to process what was happening, I crawled out of my bag and padded out into the frigid hallway, my bald head precariously close to the ceiling. Sure enough, the outside latch of Steve and Bill's room had managed to close itself just enough to keep the door from opening. I quickly unlatched it and dove back into bed, trying to recreate the dream before it faded into oblivion.

"Thanks, man!" Steve hissed as he went past our door toward the communal bathroom. "I was about to pee myself!"

FOURTEEN
GIVING UP THE GHOST

We had our usual breakfast with the entire gang the next morning, and I began to notice an uptick in the infamous Khumbu Cough, named for its prevalence among Everest trekkers and climbers. In fact, the dining area sounded like the waiting room of a walk-in clinic. The cough didn't seem to manifest until we were seated and our heart rate was at a resting pace. Then, it became a ticklish annoyance, but not much beyond that.

Holly's head cold, however, had worsened overnight and was sapping what little reserve energy she had. She and I, along with Tenzi and Hari, started out that day's trek at the same time as the rest of the group, but we were soon outpaced.

The trail continued to be fairly flat and level for the first thirty minutes before crossing the small stream and sloping up the opposite mountainside. At the top was an ancient chorten monument, and we stopped there for a short rest while I shot some video.

From here on out, the trail would run along the contours of the current mountains, with the Dudh Kosi River roaring far below us in the gorge.

At first, I was encouraged by Holly's progress. Her knees seemed to be holding up well, and she was in good spirits as we navigated around many additional chortens, stupas, and mani stone-lined walls. But as we approached Upper Pangboche for our lunch break (we didn't do our morning tea), her knees began locking up again. I could see that they were staying operable for shorter and shorter blocks of time.

We took it very slow.

The gang ascends a gentle slope on the trail to Upper Pangboche. Photo by Bill Shupp.

The group was waiting for us at a lovely place, the Himalayan Holiday Inn Trekker's Lodge. I was pretty certain it wasn't part of the Holiday Inn chain, but we played along. Overlooking yet another beautiful monastery, the lodge was tucked into the mountain, its front facing into the valley. Ama Dablam was thrusting into the clouds above. We took seats on a tile patio accompanied by a cat and two fluffy black dogs that had collapsed at our feet with giant sighs, basking in the sun's warmth.

As I enjoyed my egg sandwich, I noticed three guys walk up. One was holding an expensive-looking video camera and began filming as another interviewed the third guy. We gathered by the conversation that the guy being interviewed had taken part in a dramatic helicopter rescue on the slopes of Ama Dablam earlier in the day. Apparently, it had only recently ended.

We later found out that the interviewee was a British celebrity named Ant Middleton. He is the star of a TV program in which he embarks on various extreme survival missions with his team of sidekick dudes, all very buff and outdoorsy with beards like mine, except brown or black. Ant seemed like a likable man, and all the women in our group were immediately taken with him, including my own wife.

Just in case she was forgetting, I pointed out that she was already happily married with three children.

At the behest of the men in our group (mainly me), we left lunch a little early, anxious to get away from a clearly unfavorable (to me) comparison.

THE TRAIL FROM UPPER PANGBOCHE TO PHORTSE WAS the most beautiful but also the most difficult stretch of the entire trek. Not because the trail was particularly extreme; most of it wasn't. But there were sections of steep stone steps, mostly descents, which began to wreak havoc on Holly's knees. During the first couple of these, she went very slowly, turning her body sideways and taking one step at a time with the aid of her trekking poles. But soon, she was struggling with that method and devised a plan where she would hold onto both of my shoulders as I led her down, taking much of the weight off her knees.

It was painfully slow, and she was often in tears. As we progressed, the feeling of dread that had come on yesterday intensified.

Something would have to give, I realized. She wasn't going to make it to Lukla.

As we inched along, I tried to distract her by pointing out mountain goats on the hillsides around us., and free-grazing yaks hundreds if not thousands of feet above us. I was anxious to get past those yaks lest they kick some rocks loose. Although someday —when I'm much older—I would like to die in a heroic way, I didn't want to be taken out on this particular hillside by beasts of burden.

The trail meandered around the mountain, at times precariously close to very steep drops with the river far below. A low cloudbank hung over us for much of the afternoon and added to the otherworldly feel of the landscape. Holly improved enough to go ahead of me while I lagged behind to do some filming.

Once, I noticed movement far below and spotted a Sherpa villager peeling limbs off a small tree. Dawa explained that he was harvesting them for medicinal purposes. I can't imagine the skill it must have taken to get to where he was; it was nowhere near the relative safety of the trail.

Finally, I could see ahead that the edge of the mountain ended in a ridge, and I assumed that Phortse was on the other side. We approached the ridge to find a young girl, maybe age 8, sitting on a rock with a very young child, perhaps a toddler, in her lap, both dressed in old, oversized, heavy clothing stained from years of use. They had the ruddy cheeks and perpetually runny noses that seemed universal among Sherpa children. There were no adults in sight, but they were clearly comfortable and there on purpose. When I approached, I saw that Holly was teaching both children how to perform a high-five, much to their delight.

These two little girls charmed all of us on the trail above
Phortse. Photo by Mike Maxim.

Over the ridge lay the beautiful village of Phortse, but we
would have to navigate a steep, rutted pasture to reach the terraced
ground of the hamlet. Holly grabbed my shoulders and we moved
slowly, picking our way through the ruts and sparse vegetation.

To our utter amazement, the toddler had climbed onto her
sister's back and stuck there like a cocklebur on a dog as her
sibling bounded down the hill ahead of us, leaping from one
boulder to another. Neither one seemed the least bit concerned
and, on the contrary, were having a great time. I could tell they
were wondering why we were going so darned slow.

We finally made it into Phortse, known as "The Climber's
Village" because something like 90 percent of the households are
occupied by someone who has climbed Everest multiple times.
But the flip side of bragging rights is that whenever there is a
tragedy on the mountain involving Sherpas, they are almost
always from Phortse, making it a place of both great pride and
terrible sorrow.

Today, it was a happy place. We could see and hear children
playing outside the village school, and it made us feel a little like
we were home.

Hari and Tenzi walked ahead to alert Dawa that we had arrived in Phortse. As Holly held my arm, wincing with each step, I finally spoke the words we both knew were coming.

"This is it. We're flying you out of here."

Holly looked at me with frightened eyes.

"Really? You don't think I can make it?"

"No. I know you can't make it, and honestly, this is as bad for me as it is for you, if not worse," I said quietly. "I can't handle seeing you in such pain anymore, and even if I could, it's clear that you're done. This needs to be your last hike."

Holly's eyes filled with tears.

"Honey, let me remind you: you had less time than any of us to train," I continued. "It wasn't even close. Given the challenges you had, you should never have come, but you did it. You made it to Everest Base Camp, and that can never be taken away from you. It's a huge accomplishment and you should be nothing but proud."

As we approached Phortse Guest House, I could see Tenzi and Dawa having a serious conversation and it was clear they were discussing Holly. Dawa then met us as we reached the steps leading into the lodge.

"Are you okay?" he asked Holly with concerned eyes. "Tenzi says you had a bad struggle today."

"Yes, it's true," she replied. She took a deep breath. "I don't think I can go any farther. I think I'm done."

Dawa looked at me and I nodded in agreement.

"Let's get her out of here as soon as possible. She needs to be off her feet."

"Alright, I will go call our helicopter company from the sat phone and let Nirajann know what's happening," he said, referring to his business partner in Kathmandu. "It's too late for today, but I'm sure we can arrange something for first thing tomorrow. I'll also alert the lodge in Lukla."

All business, Dawa disappeared with his sat phone case into another room. Tenzi retrieved our room keys and, in a final cruel joke, we had to walk down a steep flight of stairs to get to our room.

That night at dinner, the announcement that Holly would be flying out the next morning was met with gasps, groans, and tears. These people, most of whom were complete strangers six months ago, had become dear friends, forever bonded through an epic shared experience that only the fifteen of us would understand, and to lose one to injury this close to the end was devastating to all.

The mood was lightened later when Dawa asked both Hari and Ngwang to give the nightly briefing. Both men, I estimated, were in their early forties, but Hari was better traveled, having spent a lot of time in Kathmandu and other cities. I suspected that Ngwang had rarely been out of the mountains, if at all. He had come a long way during the course of the trek, starting out incredibly shy, but now more confident in his English language skills.

The two were clearly terrified to get up in front of the group on their own. They presented the briefing in its entirety as if they were in a public speaking class in high school. It would appear that the fear of public speaking is universal. Both these guys could do the EBC trek blindfolded, but the formality of standing and speaking in front of the group had them in a state of near panic.

Upon completion, we gave them rousing ovations. Little Ngwang's ears reddened and he practically hid under the bill of his Hobnail cap.

It was a great end to a difficult day.

Tomorrow, however, would be one for the books.

It was an awful night's sleep for me, no doubt due more to stress than altitude. Holly had taken some pain medication for her knees that had helped her sleep, thank goodness.

In the morning, we got some comic relief provided by Holly's bedspread. Any native English-speaking person will notice that, in

Nepal, English-language renderings often go awry in translation. Holly's bedspread featured a pattern of teddy bears holding hearts under which was printed, "I love you, so thank you." As we drank our morning tea, anticipating Holly's departure, we giggled over our parting words, "I love you, so you're welcome."

Then we began the task of repacking the duffels and our backpacks, knowing that we would be spending that night apart. It was a little weird, but necessary. It was also painful to watch Holly stumbling up the flight of stairs to the dining room. That convinced me we were making the correct decision..

At breakfast, Dawa told us to be ready to go at any time because the pilot would leave Lukla as soon as the morning clouds lifted. Flying time from there to here was only about fifteen minutes. Dawa walked outside, I assumed, to make another status call to Lukla.

Meanwhile, the team gathered around Holly and wished her luck, showering her with hugs. We had no real idea of when the call would come, so Russ volunteered to hang back with Hari, Holly, and me, and hike with us after Holly left.

I had just taken my last bite of Tibetan bread when Dawa popped back into the lodge. "Okay!" he said. "Time to go! The heli is on its way!"

I grabbed the backpacks, Hari got Holly's duffel, and we headed out. Much to my chagrin, Dawa said we would have to meet the helicopter at the foot of the village on a crude heliport. It was more of a walk than I wanted my wife to make, but we had no choice.

Stretched out before us was the valley through which the aircraft would fly. What looked like a flood of white clouds was flowing through the lower part of the valley with the peaks on both sides exposed, and I hoped the pilot wouldn't have difficulty finding his way down through the soup after arriving at Lukla.

I kept that thought to myself.

"You gotta promise to do one thing," I told Holly. "As soon as you get on the chopper, start filming with your phone and don't stop until you get there. If we have to do this, we may as well get some good video out of it."

The three of us had just about made it to the landing area when the helicopter appeared suddenly. It roared over our heads, made a quick end-around turn, flew back over the pad, turned again, and settled down onto the ground. Somehow, I had the presence of mind to grab my phone out of my pocket and start filming.

One guy jumped out and ran to get Holly's bags as Hari supported her under one arm and began leading her to the craft, painted bright red and adorned with an imposing yellow dragon. I was able to give her a quick kiss and shout "I love you!" before she hobbled off with Hari as fast as her bum knees would allow.

With Hari's help, Holly limps to the helicopter as a co-pilot grabs her bags.
Photo by the author.

Before I could process what was happening, she was being helped into the chopper. The doors slammed shut and the rotors increased to full power. The craft rose about thirty feet, banked sharply to its left, and dropped off the precipice down into the valley out of sight, the distinctive whup-whup-whup sound fading to nothing almost immediately. A few seconds later, I saw it pop up over the clouds in the distance, a tiny dot framed by gigantic mountains.

Just like that, she was gone. The chopper had been on the ground for all of one minute and twenty-one seconds.

Russ and I stood there in shock, our mouths agape, as morning birds began singing again.

"Wow," was all Russ could manage. I became aware that I was out of breath, panting heavily, but not from physical exertion. The sheer intensity of watching my lovely bride whisked away on a helicopter at 11,000 feet in the Himalayas was what I can only describe as an emotional jackhammer. I was speechless.

There was nothing left to do but utter a prayer for her safe arrival in Lukla and start trekking in that direction. We turned and walked toward the mountains.

FIFTEEN

RELIEF

The evacuation had happened so fast that we were able to join up with the rest of the group as they hiked out of Phortse. Following a half-hour descent into a long gorge, we crossed yet another suspension bridge at the bottom and started back up into a pine forest.

I found myself in unfamiliar territory — near the front. The experience with the chopper had pumped me so full of adrenaline, I was worried that I might run out of steam if I didn't pace myself carefully, but it was difficult to hold back. I tried to carry on conversations, but the shock of watching the helicopter containing my wife drop off that cliff and disappear into the vast Himalayas was difficult to shake. Despite the press about the dangers of flying up here, I hadn't worried about our flight into Lukla, but this felt different.

I was officially freaked out.

Maybe it was good for me that we faced such a tough ascent early on. It was almost identical to the big push into Namche Bazaar — a powdery trail that doglegged constantly as we gained serious altitude with every step. The difference between this morning and Day 2 was that we were each now armed with millions of new microscopic porters — red blood cells — hoofing through our arteries to deliver bottles of O2 to our beleaguered circulatory systems. Even with all the pounding we'd put our bodies through, we were still superhero versions of ourselves.

Acclimatized Man: Faster than a Speeding Yak! Able to Leap Himalayan Tree Roots in a Single Bound!

After a while, our group of thirteen trekkers and five Sherpas began to stretch out like a long snake. I was still near the front. Pausing to catch my breath, I spotted Dawa far below me, near the back of the line, and yelled down to him.

"Dawa! Have you heard anything about Holly yet?"

He waved back to me with a smile.

"I just got a call from my friends in Lukla!" he yelled back up at me, cupping his hands around his mouth. "Holly arrived safely! She is in the lodge and is being taken care of!"

A cheer went up from the group, so loud that a flock of startled warblers flushed from the treetops.

Thank God!

In that moment, as if someone had just emptied my backpack, ten days of constant worry lifted from my shoulders and flew up and out of the forest along with those birds. A swell of emotion washed over me as Shari gave me a hug.

"It's okay, buddy," she said with a smile. "Holly's in good hands now."

"Yep," I replied. "Now let's climb this damn mountainside."

HOLLY HAD PUT ALL HER WEIGHT ON HARI'S ARM AS SHE half-fell into the back seat of the vibrating helicopter, moaning as pain coursed through her knees. As Hari shut the door, the Nepalese co-pilot reached back and helped buckle her in, smiling as if to say, "We can't really communicate verbally right now, so you're just going to have to trust us."

She smiled back and nodded.

Oh, my God, was all she could think.

The pilot gave her a thumbs-up and turned back to his controls.

As the RPMs began cycling up, Holly grabbed her iPhone out of her coat pocket, swiped up to reveal the camera controls, and tapped the red video record button, pointing the camera out the window. Having never been in a helicopter, she had no idea what to expect. She white-knuckled a handhold on the back of the co-pilot's chair and prayed she wouldn't puke, drop the phone, or both. Then she remembered her No-Vomiting policy and redirected all her focus on not dropping the phone.

As a surge of power lifted the craft into the sky and it began to bank left, Holly strained to see her husband on the ground below, but it was no use. The chopper turned and she felt a mild sensation of butterflies as it dropped into the valley. As the chopper locked into a proper altitude and leveled out, the butterflies fluttered back down.

"OK, this isn't terrible," she said aloud, the words heard by nobody except herself. "This is actually kind of nice."

As she filmed the hillsides and peaks rolling past beneath, disappearing into the white blanket of clouds that filled in the valley floor, a sense of peace began to come over her as she realized her trek was over. Time for healing now. Out of sheer contrary stubbornness, she had achieved her goal, Everest Base Camp. Bucket list item of fifteen years? Check. Helping and encouraging those who had entrusted their time, money, and very lives to this adventure with a company she had co-founded? Check.. She had put them first, before herself, until her knees demanded otherwise.

Then, halfway through the filming, she realized that she was holding the camera vertically. "Oh, crap. Mark's gonna kill me." Without stopping and restarting, she flipped it horizontally.

Somewhere on a mountainside behind her, Mark was rolling his eyes and feeling annoyed without knowing why.

The helicopter approached Lukla, although the village was still obscured by clouds. The pilot then began circling, looking for an opening through which to descend. It was only then that Holly's heart jumped into her throat.

What if he can't find a spot? What if he gets impatient and tries anyway?

She watched as pilot and co-pilot talked through their head-phones, gesturing and pointing. Suddenly the craft quit circling and dropped quickly. Gripping the phone in one white claw and the hand-bar in the other, Holly clenched her teeth reflexively as the chopper dropped through a perfectly helicopter-sized hole in the clouds and appeared miraculously above the 1,400-foot airstrip, moving forward to the small tarmac area. The tail end rotated and the pilot set the skids down gently.

Holly tapped off the record button just as two women approached the chopper. The older of the two, a middle-aged Sherpa, opened the door. "Are you Ms. Holly?" she asked.

"Yes! I'm so glad that . . . "

Before she could finish, the other woman, barely more than a skinny teenager, grabbed both Holly's backpack and large duffel, yanking them out of the chopper across Holly's lap. She immediately started toward an opening in the nearby chain-link fence.

"You come with me now," said the older woman, holding out her hands for support as Holly clambered out. "We will go over here."

Holly sensed she should forego questions and follow directions. Hanging onto the Sherpa, she hobbled a hundred feet to the entrance of the same teahouse, the Everest Mountain Home Lodge, where the group had staged their departure twelve days earlier. She was led to a comfortable, padded bench.

"Can you call Dawa and let them know that I'm here?" Holly asked timidly. "I'm sure my husband is worried."

The woman, clearly the manager or owner of the lodge, gave

her an unexpected but warm smile. "Yes, Ms. Holly. I will do this for you. Just relax now."

She scurried away.

AFTER CLOSE TO AN HOUR OF HARD CLIMBING, WE finally topped the ridge. Ahead on a plateau was a quaint teahouse, smaller than most, overlooking miles of valleys, rivers, and peaks. Below it were a few more scattered lodges. A sign on one read "Mongla Lodge."

I guess this was Mongla.

Maybe it was actually the mythical Shangri-La of James Hilton's novel *Lost Horizon*. Sure, we had seen a lot of villages, but very few with a view quite this remarkable.

The morning sun shone out of a brilliant blue sky, reflecting off the sea of clouds filling the valley gorges far below us.

To everyone's delight, Tenzi waved us through the opening in a stone wall and onto the patio of the place, yet another Buddha Lodge & Restaurant. After determining that it was too chilly to sit outside in our now-sweaty base layers, so we began moving inside.

Mike Maxim, aka "Tarzan," was the only one of us brave enough to strip down to his bare chest, spreading his wool t-shirt out to dry in the sun. I considered doing the same but didn't want to unnecessarily shame Mike by displaying my awesome dad-bod next to his. That's just the kind of guy I am.

Inside, the mood was light, despite the preponderance of the Khumbu Cough. The news of Holly's successful evacuation had put everyone at ease and we celebrated with hot teas, bottled waters, and Snicker bars.

Emboldened and energized, we took off down the trail. Dawa had hung a fat carrot out in front of us — a great lunch at Namche Bazaar — and it was on everyone's minds as we crossed several ridges and navigated multiple stone staircases. With each step, I thanked God for allowing Holly to be flown to Lukla. Her knees wouldn't have lasted five minutes on this leg of the trek.

We shifted our collective concern from Holly's knees to Russ's. He was taking the staircases very slowly, sideways and one at a time, often grimacing in pain. But as a veteran of six knee surgeries and dozens of obstacle races every year, Russ assured us not to worry. He would make it.

"Slowly, slowly catches the yeti," he reminded us with a laugh.

Soon, we passed the teahouse from where Holly and I had called Sam, complete with the "Paid" and "Free" toilets. We were shocked to see that in a week's time, most of a large, two-story teahouse had been framed and roofed next door. As we passed, Sherpa construction workers were climbing over it like a gaggle of fourth-graders on playground equipment.

And shortly after that, we passed the old man who maintains the trail. He shouted "Namaste" and waved, seeming to remember us. I wouldn't put it past him. These people are superhuman, after all.

We pressed on, feeling the red blood cells pulsing through our veins, pushing us faster. We cruised over the wonderful, flat section of the trail from which we had called Ava, our cell phones all dinging in celebration, it seemed, as texts and emails suddenly appeared.

Far in the distance, we spotted the Hillary Bridge spanning the Dudh Kosi River like the structures on a toy train set. It was nearly incomprehensible that we would be crossing that very bridge later this day.

I LED THE WAY FOR MUCH OF THE TREK, FEELING MY oats. It felt good to stretch out my long legs, no longer worried about overtaxing myself amid increasing altitudes. We continued to descend into thicker air and more abundant oxygen.

By 11:30 a.m., we could just make out the edges of the distinctive, bowl-shaped Namche Bazaar ahead of us and below. Our pace quickened even more.

"The horses smell the barn," I commented aloud, eliciting a combination of laughter and confused expressions.

(Note: I had to explain this old mountain-ism to my non-hick brethren. The closer you get to your destination, the faster you go.)

Finally, we started down the Evil Staircase from Hell a.k.a. the stairs at Namche. Our experience was very different this time, though. Not only were we headed down, but we were flush with the achievement of reaching EBC. As we passed hordes of struggling, gasping trekkers making their way up, it felt good to offer words of encouragement.

"You've got this!"

"Almost there!"

"You guys are doing great!"

At no point was there any inkling of smugness in our voices. Really. I promise.

As we wove through the village, I saw things in a new light. Not only had we made our destination, but I was secure in the knowledge that Holly was comfortable, undoubtedly with her feet up and digging into one of those fat puzzle books she had packed. I was enjoying Namche so much, I actually forgot about Dawa's earlier promise of a "nice lunch."

And what a surprise it was!

Tenzi, leading the group, made a sudden left and veered into a doorway of tinted glass above which was displayed a very expensive-looking sign that read "Sherpa Barista." We stumbled in behind him.

Shock.

As one, we gasped. The room was as elegant as any restaurant in Nashville. Overhead was a dark wood, coffered ceiling carefully festooned with prayer flags and lit with string lights. On an attractive laminate floor, high-backed, leather chairs were pulled up to cozy, four-top tables and booths. A glass display cabinet, situated under a large flat-screen TV with a soccer match underway, featured a bevy of baked goods. The aroma of stone-fired pizza filled the air.

Although I'm sure the staff was used to customers of our ilk, I was immediately self-conscious. We looked like refugees from the Book of Exodus — sweaty, dirty, beardy (excluding the women, of course), with greasy, plastered hair (excluding me, of course), and surely followed by a green cloud of B.O. Each of us had lost an average of fifteen pounds, we later concluded, so our clothes were hanging off us. We were a band of sunken-eyed, alpine zombies. In awe, we silently filed in and took our seats amid a cloud of yak-dung dust that swirled in the light that streaming through the windows.

Within seconds, though, the shock wore off and the excitement kicked in. An obnoxiously loud chatter arose from our crew as we congratulated each other. Even though we still had a day and a half to hike, we felt as though we had made it.

Better yet, Dawa had good news for us after speaking to the owner. He stood in front of us with a wide smile. "Okay, this lunch is your reward for a job well done," he said. "Order anything you want off the menu, even meat dishes. I can vouch for the quality of the food here, so go for it. Congratulations!"

A hearty hurrah went up. For a moment, it felt like Oktoberfest minus the splashing pints of beer.

Then came a shock: I wasn't hungry! My appetite had not fully recovered from being stunted at high altitude, so nothing looked particularly appetizing. It was maddening.

However, what did sound wonderful was a hot coffee. Upon being seated, I had immediately found myself chilled due to my sweaty base layer. I guess it had not fully dried since the morning's climb to Mongla, when in my selfless decision I had opted not to air out my shirt to avoid upstaging poor Mike with my Zeus-like upper body. Now I was paying the price.

So when the waiter (an actual employee, not one of our Sherpas) took our drink orders, I asked for a café mocha. I honestly didn't expect much, just something hot.

Shock number two.

A few minutes later, the waiter placed my coffee in front of me. It was poured into a large glass rather than a mug and had a perfect cream heart crafted on the top. Although my first sip turned the perfect heart into an upside-down human butt, I took a photo before doing any more damage.

At the risk of placing a mere cup of joe on a pedestal, I nonetheless have to say . . . it was the greatest single beverage I've ever had. It felt as if Willie Wonka and Juan Valdez had conspired to brew this coffee specifically for me, using only the world's finest cocoa and coffee beans harvested by the top Oompa Loompas and . . . er . . . Juan Valdez employees.

As I took the first few luxurious sips, my chilled bones were warmed as if by a heated blanket. Eyes closed in ecstasy, I sat there in Sherpa Barista having the equivalent of a Big O as my co-trekkers uncomfortably looked in other directions.

Although I managed to choke down a fantastic salami club sandwich, it couldn't touch the sublime quality of that café mocha. Most of the team had ordered impressive pizzas, and the room echoed the sounds of others having similar Os.

An hour later, the Hobnail Trekking team strolled out of Sherpa Barista with dreamy looks on our faces, smoking imaginary cigarettes.

SIXTEEN

THE JOHNSON COMPOUND

It was time for the second leg of our day's trek — the descent to Monzo.

Even though it would be another fairly long haul, I think all of us were happy to take on the infamous Namche Bazaar climb from the other direction.

Before leaving, we arranged to meet at the foot of the village after a brief shopping excursion. There was a large construction project going on, so the few of us who arrived first took a load off and watched the proceedings.

Soon after, everyone showed up with their "shoppings" and we began threading our way through the yak, dzo, and mule trains, and the exhausted trekkers entering the village.

"Looking good!" we encouraged. "Almost there!"

I didn't have the heart to warn them about the Evil Staircase from Hell.

We continued out of the village and into the forest. I was surprised to see that we detoured onto an alternate trail that runs above the one we had used on the way up. This dramatically cut down on the two-way traffic.

Within thirty minutes we found ourselves at the Hillary Bridge. I let most of the group cross ahead of me so I could shoot GoPro footage.

We then scuttled down another ten-minute descent before the trail bottomed out in the boulder-strewn valley alongside the river. This section reminded me of any number of rivers in Colorado and Montana, and we had a good time chatting and shooting more photos and video.

As we hiked, dark gray clouds rolled in and started spitting rain at us. We stopped, spent another ten minutes digging around in our packs for rain shells, put them on, and started again.

Luis enjoys a moment of rest in the sunshine near the entrance of Namche Bazaar. Photo by the author.

Aaaaannd then the sun came back out.

We stripped the shells off and began the short but challenging incline that led us out of the national park. I felt a pang of sadness as we exited through the ornate pagoda.

When would I be back here next?

THE HOBNAIL GROUP WALKED INTO MONZO AT AROUND 3 p.m. This was our last stop before the final push into Lukla tomorrow, and there was a definite excitement in the air. As much as we had enjoyed this incredible adventure, we were all anxious for contact with the outside world. I, of course, wanted to get back to my hobbled bride.

After enjoying afternoon tea and placing our dinner orders, we adjourned to our respective rooms. This was a three-story lodge, and to my surprise, I was the only person assigned to the third floor. It seemed strangely quiet and a little creepy in the expansive hallway as I fumbled with my skeleton key. I half expected to look up and see twin little girls standing at the end of the hallway. Or maybe Jack Nicholson.

I got the door open and was unprepared for what I saw. The room was gi-NORMOUS. It had two single beds and one double bed, and was clearly meant to be a family room. The walls were painted an interesting lavender color and the view looked out over the adjacent mountain, now mostly covered in a rainy cloud. Amazingly, the room was well lit and there was a fully functioning electrical outlet on the wall! I was so excited, I dropped my duffel and backpack and immediately shot a video of the place.

I was also very nervous. Dawa informed us that assuming there was any left, we might be able to enjoy a shower with hot water. It had been nine long days since I'd had a shower on the afternoon of Day 3, and the mere thought of situating myself under hot water was intoxicating. I would take no chances by letting others go first.

It was every stinky trekker for himself!

I quickly stripped and tiptoed into the bathroom, which was adorned with strange, plastic, floral wallpaper. I could've cared less had the walls been covered in posters of a parrot sitting on a bunny sitting on a monkey holding a mango sitting on an elephant.

There was one of these in Phortse and I'm sure a hallucinogen must have been involved, possibly paired with a Pink Floyd album.

Anyway, Dawa had advised us that we may have to let the tap run for a good bit before the hot water, if there was any, would reach us. I turned the left knob clockwise . . . and a weak dribble of cold water leaked out of the shower head.

This wasn't off to a good start. Showering in this would be like having an old man peeing on my head, except without the warmth.

In a repeat of my failed shower incident in Namche, I danced back and forth on my toes in the cold bathroom, jabbing my fingers at the frigid stream and repeating a very lame prayer that went something like this: "Please God Please God Please God Please God. . . . "

Cold. Cold. Cold.

Finally, after at least five minutes, I turned off the dribble and stared at the faucets. Hmm. It couldn't hurt to try the other knob, right?

I turned it clockwise and to my surprise, a strong stream shot out of the shower head.

My hopes jumped. Could it be barely possible that whoever installed this shower switched the hot and cold knobs?

I jabbed at the water.

Cold.

Jabbed again.

Slightly less cold.

Again.

Tepid.

Could it be? CAN IT BE?

IT IS!!!!

Steaming hot water erupted from the shower, filling the room with a dense cloud. Hollering like a drunken cowboy, I jumped in the shower stall, nearly scalding myself until I could add a little cold to the mix. Immediately, I realized that Holly had taken the soap with her.

Not a problem.

Simply standing under a hot blast of water was all I needed. Between this and the café mocha at Sherpa Barista, I had experienced the most epic luxuries the world could possibly offer one less-than-epic guy.

DINNER THAT NIGHT WAS CHICKEN SOUP, ESSENTIALLY the dry mix you get out of a tin-foil package, but that was fine. Most of the gang had partaken in the same shower adventure I had, so spirits were running high. After writing my trip notes and receiving my Nalgene bottle of boiling water, I excused myself and headed to Casa De Johnson, sometimes known as the Johnson Compound.

Ah, the luxury of it all.

After careful deliberation (about two seconds), I chose to retire to the double bed rather than one of the singles, of course. Propped up on several pillows, I put my iPad on my chest and watched most of a documentary about Antarctica, which made my present location seem balmy by comparison. Finally getting sleepy at around 11 p.m., I shut it all down and fell asleep.

Uh, oh.

I knew there was a problem before I even opened my eyes. I could feel my throat trying to reflexively swallow and every time it did, there was pain. My sinuses felt horrible — tingling with needles — and my temples were throbbing.

I rolled over the looked at my phone. It was 12:45 a.m.

Turning onto my other side, I tried to ignore my condition and go back to sleep.

Yeah, that's right… This is all just a bad dream.

Nope.

I sat up in the dark. Pounding. Nose running.

I clambered for the handkerchief that was still in the pocket of my hiking pants.

Lie back down. Ignore this. Ignore this.

Nope.

Back up.

Never in my life can I recall such an intense sinus infection, if that's what it was, coming on so quickly.

Dang. I knew this room was too good to be true. Maybe the Trekking Gods were punishing me for not having turned in my key to Tenzi and admitting he had given me the wrong room. Or maybe the Shower Gods were mad at me for using up too much hot water. Or maybe it was the Café Mocha Gods.

Someone was clearly punishing me for something.

All night long, I sat in the darkness, propped up with the handkerchief in my hand, occasionally dozing off until the excruciating pain in my nose jolted me awake again.

How could I hike like this tomorrow?

How??

BY 6:30 A.M., I COULDN'T DO IT ANYMORE. UNDER NO circumstances could I get comfortable in my bag. Sleep was impossible.

I crawled out, packed up, and headed downstairs to the dining room. As they filtered in, the gang was horrified to see my face, which looked like Picasso had painted it various shades of red and re-arranged it. I nibbled at breakfast before giving up.

It actually felt a little better to be walking on the trail, although the energy I had experienced yesterday had drained out through my toes during the night. I trudged along in the back of the group, lagging behind.

We stopped for tea at Ngwang's house and he was excited to show us around and introduce us to his sweet wife and twelve-year-old son, Pemba. The family dog, a shaggy dude appropriately named "Happy," greeted all of us individually, but favored Stefanie, Shari, and Gina, clearly pushovers.

Ngwang's little teahouse was tiny but neat and well organized. The main room had a low ceiling with exposed pine beams, rough-hewn hardwood floors, and shelving units built into two corners, all stacked high with carefully folded sleeping bags, comforters, and other trekking supplies. As with all teahouses, there was bench seating around the perimeter of the room facing long wooden tables. Sometimes there were chairs on the other side of the tables, sometimes not.

An entrance to the kitchen was covered by a hanging tapestry, and we could hear Ngwang, his wife, and Tenzi chatting happily as they prepared our teas. Upon serving us, Ngwang formally welcomed us to his home, leaving many of us misty-eyed.

(I was already a mess, so nobody would have known the difference.)

IT WAS A WONDERFUL WAY TO SPEND THE MORNING OF our last day on trek, and I was perturbed that I couldn't enjoy it more. I generally kept to myself and tried to control the constant ocean tide of pain that rhythmically rose and fell in my sinuses. The tea had no taste. Even as I write this, I wish I could pick up the phone, call Ngwang, and apologize for my demeanor that day. Among my many future goals is to return to the Yak Man's home in good health, and to share laughs, stories, and dal bhat.

After saying our goodbyes, we headed out again and quickly turned right off of the main trail. This was the detour — an insider's special — that Dawa had promised for our group.

Even in my current condition, honking and snorting like some curmudgeonly rhinoceros, I would count this section of the trail as my favorite. In some ways, it was comparable to leaving Mt. Doom in the Black Land of Mordor and returning to the Shire. (Yes, I'm a Lord of the Rings geek.)

The author and Ngwang, the yak man. I'll let you determine who is who. Photo by Holly Johnson.

In contrast to the harsh, monotone, lunar landscape of Everest — devoid of all life save for its human visitors and a few insane birds — we were now walking along a stone-wall-lined path through lush farmland pulsing with growth. We passed fields of buckwheat, barley, millet, and rice, creating a crazy palette of greens. Other fields served as pasture ground, with small, open-sided shelters under which lay young dzo calves, staring at us as we passed.

Occasionally, we would leave the farms and move across rocky areas, usually a dry creek bed, and then skirt slightly up along the edges of a forest before dropping back down into the valley. The Dudh Kosi roared alongside the entire time, providing a pleasant white noise that only added to the ambiance.

For a good half-hour we were adopted by a friendly farm dog who took it upon himself to escort us through his countryside. Not interested in being petted, he was all about his guiding business, pausing only to pee at strategic places and kick soil over his offending spot and whoever happened to be walking past at the moment. At some point along the way, he decided the bumbling humans could make it from there on out and he peeled off, wagging his tail in salute before disappearing.

As we traveled, I was both miserable and enchanted. I tried desperately to ignore my pounding head and weakened legs to commit the experience to my memory.

I took it slow out of necessity and fell behind most of the group except for Bill and Mike, who were concentrating on photography, and Tenzi and Dawa, who were probably afraid that I might snort and cough myself blind, take a wrong turn, and end up in Tibet. Can't say I blamed them.

We crossed a gleaming, recently-constructed suspension bridge and meandered into a familiar-looking village. Sadly, our detour ended when the trail teed into the main route. We hung a right and continued on, until stopping for lunch in Phakding at the same teahouse, Namaste Lodge, where we'd slept the first night. I forced myself to eat a bowl of powdered chicken noodle soup, not that I could taste anything.

As I sat there, I felt stress creeping up on me, either worry about Holly or my last stretch of the trek. I knew we had a long uphill hike from here on out, three to four hours, and I was concerned about actually making it to Lukla.

Would they have to airlift me, too?

I looked around at our team and made a mental inventory. Natalie had contracted a sinus infection almost at the very beginning, and it lasted days, but she was laughing with Stefanie, clearly happy. She had taken control of her condition; not the other way around.

Shari had suffered through food poisoning or something similar during the night at Tengboche. At the time, I was afraid she wouldn't continue on, but after a day and a half, she was back at 100 percent and powered up to Base Camp.

Luis had opted not to take Diamox, attempting to complete the trek entirely naturally, much to his credit. A gifted athlete and extremely competitive, the scuba diver/polo player/ hiker had pushed a little too hard at the beginning and by our acclimatization hike at Namche, he was feeling it. He spent the next several days fighting nausea and lack of energy, but a late round of Diamox finally knocked out most of his symptoms and he rebounded.

Gina, bless her heart, experienced two days of dysentery at the highest altitudes, but with the help of physician's assistants Shari and Rachel stayed hydrated and fought through it, arriving back in Phakding at nearly full strength.

Now, here we were, less than four hours left in our journey. Through bleary eyes, I stared out the window at the mountains.

How would this thing end for me?

SEVENTEEN

A DIVINE FINAL PUSH

W e were off again. Our last stop would be a short tea break in two hours.

I moved along down the trail awkwardly, no longer using my trekking poles in favor of keeping my hands shoved into my jacket pockets where they seemed more comfortable. It had rained the previous night and the usually dusty trail had been transformed into slippery muck in many places, but I didn't care. I slogged through it all, hacking and sneezing, as Dawa kept a concerned watch over me.

The tea stop was little more than a blur, and I can't recall what flavor I chose or how much I drank. I was in survival mode, concerned only with placing one boot in front of the other. The epic Himalayan landscape flaunted itself before me, vying for my attention, but I was having none of it.

I decided to try to keep pace with the front-runners just to distract myself, so I caught up with Mike, Stefanie, Shari, and Steve. I walked alongside them in silence, listening to their conversations. About halfway up a long incline, Tenzi pulled us over for a rest stop.

"Water break, everyone!" he shouted down the trail. The trekkers dutifully paused and began slipping out of their packs.

Oddly, I didn't feel like stopping.

"Dawa, is it OK if I keep going?" I asked. "I've got a little momentum and better take advantage of it up this hill."

He looked at me with a sideways glance.

"Sure, okay."

"I'd like to keep going too, if that's okay," Mike chimed in.

"So would I," said both Stefanie and Shari in unison.

"Yep, y'all go ahead," Dawa said. "We'll catch up in a few minutes."

The four of us continued up the slope with me in the lead.

Then it happened.

As we reached a plateau near the top, a feeling swept through my battered, sick, fifty-two-year-old body that I can only describe as . . . power.

Without conscious thought, my stride lengthened to a walking pace that I had not yet experienced. My hands popped out of my jacket pockets and began swinging in rhythm. My ragged breathing formed a cadence, working itself into the alternating clip-clops of my boots like the perfect kick-drum backbeat in a funk song.

I felt the distance between myself and my small group of co-hikers widening. Their conversation was getting more distant as my pace grew faster and faster. Finally, I heard Mike Maxim's voice.

"He's in a zone," he said to Stefanie and Shari. "He's gone."

And I was.

The ground began flying past me and my ears filled with a combination of wind and the rhythm of my breathing. One by one and group by group, I began passing the traffic on the trail ahead of me. On the entire trek I don't think I'd passed a single person— quite to the contrary, I was usually the one being passed. But now, trekkers were dropping past me in droves.

Still, I went faster.

Then, I began passing Sherpa porters. Then, mule and yak trains.

Nobody on this trail was traveling faster than me.

My mind swirled with possible explanations, but only one made sense: Call it whatever, but a Divine energy had found its way into my body, driving me to my wife and gifting me the last two hours of this adventure. My worry about Holly, the health of our trekkers, and the success of the trip were all behind me now.

God had dropped an unlikely opportunity in my lap two years earlier when He put me in that little red Nissan with Dawa, giving me the idea to start a business. All of those months of planning . . . naming the company, building a website, reading books and watching videos, purchasing gear we couldn't afford, having the unmitigated gall to speak in front of strangers about a trip I'd never experienced in a country I'd never visited, forming a partnership with a guy I hardly knew, leaving our three children parentless for three weeks, and being wracked with worry about my wife and every one of our thirteen new and old friends . . . had all built up to this moment.

For the next two hours, I would transform from being a Pitiful-Sinus-Infected-Bleary-Eyed-Leaden-Legged Doofus Dad into a strapping 8-cylinder, turbo-driven, off-road, God-Almighty-fueled monster truck.

I sped on, neither stopping nor even slowing down for rest breaks at the tops of the many inclines I ascended.

It all became a blur and I honestly can't remember most of it. But I do recall rounding a curve and coming up on a team of dzos at the base of a steep staircase.

The dzos looked familiar. They were ours. Ngwang was walking alongside them. I flew past on my way up, and upon recognizing our yak man, turned around and shouted "Namaste" without breaking stride. Ngwang's eyes got huge and his mouth dropped open. With one arm, he flexed his biceps in the classic muscle-man pose.

"Strong man!" he shouted and pointed at me.

That might've been the greatest compliment I've ever received.

I pressed on up the hill.

By now, my heavy breathing had become very loud, like the huffing of a threatened grizzly bear, no doubt disconcerting for the people I was passing. My face was surely beet red against my gigantic buff-beard, blowing sideways in the wind. I can imagine I made quite a sight.

This was confirmed when I rounded a bend and crossed a short bridge just as a Sherpa mother holding the hand of a young child stepped onto the span from the other direction. The woman appeared startled by my appearance, and the child cowered behind her.

"Namaste!" I shouted through my huffing, trying to diffuse their obvious concern as I passed them.

"Namaste," the woman repeated back to me with a look of shock. "Wow!"

It wasn't a word I would have expected to hear from a Sherpa. I laughed to myself and kept going.

Not long after, I looked up and saw the village of Lukla on the ridge ahead of me. All that was left was that first, long, downward slope we had navigated upon leaving twelve days ago. Only now, it was a long UP. Then, I would have the hike through Lukla itself.

I could feel my supernatural power starting to falter slightly, so I gave that last climb everything I had, exhaling in mighty breaths like an Old West freight train powering up a steep section of Colorado track.

Suddenly, gasping in great moans, I was at the top and standing at the entrance to Lukla. All that remained was the distance to the lodge. Holly was less than five minutes away and had absolutely no idea where I was or when I would be showing up. She knew nothing about my sinus infection.

I stood erect and powered my boots forward again, picking up speed through the village.

The last incline of my entire three-week adventure in Nepal was the staircase climb around the top of the Lukla airstrip. I gave it all I had, and then suddenly, it was over. I was heading down and the lodge was in sight.

I passed the airport entrance, took the lodge steps two at a time, and burst in the front door, scanning the room for Holly.

She was right there, seated on the bench nearest the door, feet up, puzzle book in her hand. She glanced up at the noise of the opening door and our eyes met.

The puzzle book dropped to the floor with a soft clatter.

ACCORDING TO MY PHONE, I HAD CREATED A FORTY-minute gap between myself and the next closest Hobnail hikers. That was good because I needed most of that time to recover.

After our initial embrace, I collapsed into a chair beside Holly, every last itty-bitty bit of energy in my body gone, all of it left on the trail. God had seen fit to give me that mystical, healing power for two hours, and then He said, "That's enough. You're done for a while. And oh, by the way, you still have that sinus infection."

C'mon, God!

I had just enough strength to stand outside with Holly and film our gang as they made their final steps into the lodge entrance. With each team member came a barrage of hugs and high-fives along with a few tears.

When we were all accounted for, the team hung out in the dining room as Dawa figured up how much each member should tip our Sherpa guys. We then received our room keys and headed to our rooms.

(Note: Tips turned out to be around $50 USD per trekker, which was universally perceived as an absurd bargain.)

Monster truck no more—the wheels had come off, and all that

was left of my legs were thin rubber. Holly could barely walk on her swollen knees. We shuffled our way outside like a couple of ninety-year-olds, climbed ONE step into the hallway of the lodge, and made our way to the room Holly had occupied since yesterday. Once inside, it was nap time for me immediately while my lovely wife picked up where she left off in her puzzle book.

She roused me an hour later, and if anything, I felt worse. My sinus had reached Epic-ly Crappy Proportions. (You know it's bad when you have to make up a word to describe it.)

In the dim dining room of Everest Mountain Home Lodge, we partook of our last supper — on trek, that is — after which speeches were made. Mike presented the tips to the Sherpas, one at a time, to crazy applause as the recipient circled the room, shaking our hands or hugging us one at a time.

For days, I had been planning my emotional, inspirational, tear-jerking, Academy-Award-Winning, end-of-trek speech. But now, I couldn't croak out two words without being thrown into a spasm of violent sneezing and disgusting nose-blowing. I turned the speech-making duties over to Holly and retreated to a dark corner so as not to gross everybody out.

She had us all in tears, of course.

Afterward, Holly and I made our apologies and retired early, sad that we would miss a dance party that was planned for later. From the look of things, we would be the only ones not in attendance.

We waddled back to our room. After both of us popped Tylenol PMs, Holly and I crawled into our respective sleeping bags, shut off the lights, and settled in, me with a final sleepy sneeze.

Silence.

BOOM. *BA-BOOM BOOM*. BOOM. *BA-BOOM BOOM*.

The window creaked slightly, vibrating with each BOOM of a kick drum.

BOOM. *BA-BOOM BOOM*. BOOM. *BA-BOOM BOOM*.

The container of Tylenol PM, powered by the vibrations, walked its way across the end table and clattered to the floor.

The dance party was clearly underway.

"Oh, my God," Holly said in the darkness.

We then broke into hoarse, Khumbu Cough inducing giggles until the sleepy part of the medicine kicked in and we both dozed off in spite of the techno-Sherpa-dance party raging only feet away.

EIGHTEEN

EXCITEMENT AND REGRET

The Hobnail group entered the Lukla airport terminal at around 7:00 a.m. Even first thing in the morning, it was a jumbled crush of backpacks, duffel bags, Sherpas, and adventurers, over which hung with a cloud of body odor reminiscent of the smog over L.A. In silent judgment, we glanced sideways at each other with crinkled noses.

Again, I was incredibly thankful for Dawa and Tenzi, who were both handling all of the logistics of the flight. All we had to do was stand in a smelly huddled line, waiting for someone to tell us what to do and where to go.

Eventually, we were directed down a flight of steps and through the security protocol, which oddly consisted of separate metal detectors for men and women. Holly is still convinced that the women's metal detector was not actually plugged in — probably broken — but they were made to walk through it anyway. At one point, I was sure I heard a gate agent yell "BEEP!" in a falsetto voice out of the corner of his mouth and then make a woman walk through again.

We ended up at the "gate," which was not much larger than a

doctor's waiting room. There, Holly and I sat slumped in molded plastic chairs.

We made a fine pair, she with her swollen knees; me with my swollen head. In spite of her disability, Holly still fulfilled her responsibilities as Brains of the Operation for the Johnsons, going over our schedule for the rest of the day and making sure I'd had my medicine.

"Yes, excuse me?" Tenzi shouted after half an hour. "Time to go! Follow me, please!"

We shuffled out onto the tarmac. Our Summit Airlines airplane, engines still whining, was being de-boarded with fresh, clean-shaven, perfect-hair-having trekkers. Their smiles slanted downward, eyes widening, as they passed the odorous alpine zombies moving in the opposite direction.

"Good job." we intoned reflexively.

"You got this."

"Not much further."

The new trekkers stared at us and picked up their pace, scurrying past.

We boarded the plane with fresh excitement. We had landed at the World's Most Dangerous Airport, and now, we would get to take off from here. As we climbed in, the same flight attendant from our inbound trip directed us to our places. Oddly, she again singled out Kathy to sit beside her in the rear two seats.

Within minutes, the engines began powering up and we taxied out to the end of the airstrip, did a 180-degree turn, and stopped. I could see people filming us from the trail and had black thoughts about whether they would be recording our demise, but quickly dismissed the notion.

Everyone had their phones and GoPros out inside the cabin, too. There was a whine of increasing RPMs and we felt the brakes release. The airplane began rolling as we all shouted with various "Here we go!" and "Oh, boy!" and "Hold on!" comments.

The wheels left the pavement just as we hit the painted stripes at the end of the airstrip and then the ground fell away. We were immediately over a deep gorge.

"Woo-hoo!" the passengers all yelled in unison.

Then we fell silent, and I had the distinct feeling that our team members were all saying their quiet, personal goodbyes to the towering peaks, clanking yaks, and wonderful Sherpas who had been our gracious hosts for the past two weeks.

The plane banked over the ridges and headed southwest.

KATHY WAS FILMING THE TERRACED LANDSCAPE underneath when the flight attendant tapped her shoulder.

"Please?" the attendant said, holding out her iPhone to Kathy, the camera app active on the screen.

Kathy took the phone, confused. The attendant, a twenty-something, heavily made-up girl, immediately struck a pose, looking at the camera with duck lips.

"Oh," Kathy said as the realization set in. She tried to compose the photo correctly and snapped a couple of frames, handing the phone back.

The girl waved the phone away, motioning for Kathy to take more pictures.

"Ooh-kay," said the South Carolinian, too shocked and bumfuddled to question the young woman.

Click, click, click.

The attendant shifted in the chair, put a hand under her chin, and looked contemplatively into an imagined distance.

Click, click, click, went the camera app.

Now, she was laughing, enjoying her flight-attendant lifestyle.

Click, click, click.

No, flip the phone over and shoot vertically. Now, hold it up high and shoot down.

Click, click, click.

This continued for the entirety of the forty-five-minute flight, adding a bizarre exclamation point to an otherwise awesome experience. If this girl ever lands a gig with a modeling agency, poor over-worked Kathy deserves a cut of the royalties.

~

I SPENT MOST OF THE FLIGHT BACK THE SAME WAY WE all did (except Kathy) — silently peering out the window at the receding mountains. My excitement of seeing our kids and eating a Wendy's Baconator cheeseburger was almost overpowered by the regret I felt as I watched the peaks getting smaller. It was far too soon to look back on the adventure with any real clarity and understanding; we were still reeling from exhaustion and sensory overload and had to stay in the moment as we navigated our way home through a variety of airports, layovers, sleepless flights, and crowded baggage claims. Yes, I would soon be stumbling through an airport, handing incorrect documents to impatient gate agents, annoying security personnel, and generally doing it all wrong.

I tried desperately to take it in, that we had walked in the footsteps of the world's greatest heroes, lived with Sherpa supermen and women, and viewed the top of the world with our own eyes.

Grasping for straws, I looked around for a lasting impression that would be forever imprinted in my memory. I glanced back toward the back of the plane and noticed Kathy taking odd photos of the flight attendant seated next to her.

No, that's weird, erase that vision. That can't be your lasting memory.

I turned to look out the window again just as the last snow-capped peak disappeared behind a smaller, green one in the foreground.

It would have to do. Somewhere in my brain, a shutter release clicked and the image burned itself into my mind.

I smiled, sat back in my seat, and closed my eyes, hoping to get a little shut-eye as *Ka-Ka-Ka*-Kathmandu appeared on the horizon.

EPILOGUE

Despite my head cold and Holly's inability to walk, our last two days in Kathmandu were wonderful. We spent most of the time lounging around the Hotel Tibet, either in our room or at the Yeti Bar & Terrace. We answered emails, posted photos on our Hobnail Trekking Co. social media pages, and communicated with friends and family back home.

The final evening prior to the group flying out the next morning, we met at a nice restaurant and enjoyed a last meal together. The next morning was tough, though, because it was time to bid farewell to our Sherpas. We were unprepared for how close we had grown to these guys, and there wasn't a dry eye in the house as we hugged them goodbye. It's difficult to part ways with a friend you may never see again, even for a hardened, emotionally stunted, tough guy like me.

(Don't be fooled. I cry at the end of "Monsters, Inc.")

Soon, we were once again milling around Tribhuvan International Airport, purchasing odd candies and cappuccinos while we waited for our first flight. I was relieved when the plane left the ground, half expecting a Nepalese Customs agent to rush onto the cabin and force me to pay more ransom for all those sneakers.

THE NEXT NIGHT, APRIL 15, WE LANDED IN NASHVILLE AT around 11:45 p.m. As we had done in both China and Los Angeles, I tracked down a gate agent immediately upon entering the terminal and requested a wheelchair for Holly and her inflamed knees. This was, of course, mortifying for her, especially when she was parked beside a row of elderly people waiting for early boarding. She tried to slump down into the chair and hide behind her sunglasses.

For me, though, it worked out quite well, because traveling with a disabled person comes with perks, mainly in the boarding and immigration process. I don't mean to be flippant — it's just true. Clearly, it meant we were in the first boarding group, but when we arrived in Los Angeles, having Holly in a wheelchair was like carrying a Golden Ticket. The wheelchair wrangler who was assigned to us, an older Hispanic gentleman, became our own personal airport Sherpa. He knew exactly where to go, including the shortcuts, which line to join, and most importantly, how to work the Customs kiosk.

Plus, he was fast. I was practically running to keep up with him as he raced Holly through the airport.

Best of all, this guy drained off all my airport stress; I didn't have to think about anything, just keep up.

The flights had been very much the same as they were on the way out — Holly snoozed while I watched movies and tried not to develop blood clots. Even after the events of the past three weeks, I couldn't get any decent sleep. I used every combination of neck pillow and eye mask I could think of, to no avail.

"You shall not sleep!" Gandolf the Grey shouted in my mind, his staff raised menacingly. And so it was.

The final indignity occurred at the end of our last flight. We were squeezed, quite literally, into the absolute last row of seats on the airplane, so the backs wouldn't recline much at all. Resigned to my fate, I finished the previous movie on my iPad, another documentary, and started the John Krasinski picture "Thirteen Hours: The Secret Soldiers of Benghazi." As the gripping tale of heroism was reaching its climax, I glanced outside and saw the lights of Nashville approaching.

Crap! Hurry up, movie!

Bang-bang-bang! John Krasinski, injured and almost out of options, was shooting the bad guys and tossing grenades in one final desperate stand, the soundtrack swelling in my ear buds.

"Alright, you suckers!" John Krasinski yelled as the bad guys rushed him. "Say hello to my little fri . . . "

"Sir, I have to ask you to turn off your electronics for landing," the flight attendant said, making me jump and nearly drop the iPad onto the floor.

%^#&!*

I closed the iPad and sighed. *(The next day, I retreated to my bedroom and opened up Netflix, excited to finish the movie. It had expired. As I'm writing this, it's three months later and I still don't know if John Krasinski survived or not.)*

AFTER BEING UBERED TO WHERE WE HAD STASHED OUR vehicle, Holly and I made the forty-five-minute drive home. It was now nearly 1:00 a.m. and I hadn't slept more than ten minutes at a time for something like thirty-six hours. Even with the excitement of seeing our kids, who were waiting up for us, I struggled to keep my eyes open during the last mile. I was determined not to die five minutes from home after traveling halfway around the world. Of all the doofus things I could do, that would be the worst.

We were greeted with three of the best hugs I could ever imagine. Even in our state of extreme sleep deprivation (me, not Holly), we sat up for an hour with the kids, distributing souvenirs, telling stories, and making sure the house hadn't been flooded.

As I gleefully crawled into my own, wonderful bed, I drifted off to sleep smiling, wondering when I would experience the soaring Himalayas again and what improbable adventure I would stumble into next.

APPENDIX A — ITINERARY AND TREKKING STATISTICS

The following represents a fairly typical itinerary for the Everest Base Camp trek. Variations are usually related to the Dingboche to Lobuche route (some people stay in Pheriche on the way up) and the Day 11 route (some go from Pheriche to Tengboche rather than Phortse). My advice is to try to vary your trek back as much as possible so that you're not always covering the same ground.

If you're traveling with a company like Hobnail, your teahouses are usually booked in advance, which allows you to pre-design your itinerary. If you're traveling on your own, you may have to make last-minute decisions on your route based on lodging availability. At the very least, I strongly recommend trekking with a seasoned, local guide. This is a safe trip, but on the rare occasion that someone gets into trouble, it's almost always a lone, unguided trekker.

The stats are based on our experience and are entirely unscientific, so don't reference them in a scholarly paper or anything. I believe they're fairly accurate, though, and should serve you well.

2018 EBC HOBNAIL TREKKING ITINERARY

Day 1, March 30.   Arrival in Kathmandu and transfer to Hotel Tibet.

Day 2, March 31.   Flight from Kathmandu to Lukla, trek to Phakding, Namaste Lodge.

Day 3, April 1.   Phakding to Namche Bazaar, Green Tara Resort.

Day 4, April 2.   Day of acclimatization at Namche Bazaar, Green Tara Resort.

Day 5, April 3.   Namche Bazaar to Tengboche, Tengboche Guest House.

Day 6, April 4.   Tengboche to Dingboche, Peaceful Lodge & Restaurant.

Day 7, April 5.   Day of acclimatization in Dingboche, Peaceful Lodge & Restaurant.

Day 8, April 6.   Dingboche to Lobuche, Himalayan Chain Resort Eco Lodge.

Day 9, April 7.   Lobuche to Gorak Shep to Everest Base Camp, Buddha Lodge.

Day 10, April 8.   Gorak Shep to Kala Patthar to Pheriche, Pheriche Resort.

Day 11, April 9.   Pheriche to Phortse, Phortse Guest House.

Day 12, April 10.   Phortse to Monzo, Mt. Kailash Lodge.

Day 13, April 11.   Monzo to Lukla, Everest Mountain Home.

Day 14 April 12.   Flight to Kathmandu, Hotel Tibet.

Day 15, April 13.   Free day at Kathmandu, Hotel Tibet.

Day 16, April 14.   Final departure.

2018 EBC TREKKING STATISTICS

Day 1: Lukla to Phakding
Starting elevation: 9,301'
Finishing elevation: 8,698'
Hiking distance: 4 miles
Hiking time: 4-5 hours

Day 2: Phakding to Namche Bazaar
Starting elevation: 8,698'
Finishing elevation: 11,283'
Hiking distance: 6 miles
Hiking time: 6 hours

Day 3: Acclimatization Hike
Highest elevation reached: 13,000'
Hiking distance: 4 miles
Hiking time: 4 hours

Day 4: Namche Bazaar to Tengboche
Starting elevation: 11,283'
Finishing elevation: 12,664'
Hiking distance: 5.72 miles
Hiking time: 4 hours

Day 5: Tengboche to Dingboche
Starting elevation: 12,664'
Ending elevation: 14,444'
Hiking distance: 4.5 miles
Hiking time: 4 hours

Day 6: Acclimatization Hike
Highest elevation: 14, 950'
Hiking distance: 2 miles
Hiking time: 3 hours

Day 7: Dingboche to Lobuche
Starting elevation: 14,444'
Finishing elevation: 16,400'
Hiking distance: 4 miles
Hiking time: 6.5 hours

Day 8: Lobuche to Gorak Shep to EBC
Starting elevation: 16,400'
Highest elevation: 17,599'
Sleeping elevation: 17,060
Hiking distance: 5 miles
Hiking time: 7-8 hours

Day 9: Gorak Shep to Pheriche
Starting elevation: 17,060'
Kalapathar summit: 18,006'
Finishing destination: 14,340'
Hiking distance: 8 miles
Hiking time: 8-9 hours

Day 10: Pheriche to Phortse
Starting elevation: 14,340'
Finishing elevation: 12,959'
Hiking distance: 7 miles
Hiking time: 5-6 hours

Day 11: Phortse to Monzo
Starting elevation: 12,959'
Finishing elevation: 9,301'
Hiking distance: 8 miles
Hiking time: 7-8 hours

Day 12: Monzo to Lukla
Starting elevation: 9,301'
Finishing elevation: 9,383'
Hiking distance: 4 miles
Hiking time: 3-4 hours

APPENDIX B — GEAR

As you can imagine, gear is Kind of a Big Deal when trekking in Nepal. Although you can purchase much of it more affordably in Kathmandu and along the trek itself rather than in the U.S., certain conditions must be in place for this to work out.

First, you can't be a lumbering giant like me. You probably won't find stuff in Nepal that fits you. If you are a normal-sized human being, you will be fine. There are a zillion gear shops in Kathmandu, Lukla, and Namche Bazaar for ordinary mortals.

Second, if your training takes place over the wintertime in the U.S., like it did for us, you'll probably need a lot of your gear before you ever get to Nepal. However, if most of your training is in warm weather, then no problem; get your cold weather gear in Nepal if you want.

Keep in mind that although the gear may have recognizable brand names and logos, they are likely to be knock-offs (that's why they're so cheap). But they will probably work just fine.

Also make a note that there are weight restrictions for your duffel bag and backpack when flying from Kathmandu to Lukla. Currently, your duffel must be less than 22 pounds fully packed.

Your backpack must be under 11 pounds. A helpful trick is, when you arrive for your flight, wear as much clothing and heavy stuff on your body as possible to lighten the load in your bags.

The following documents contain the gear that Holly and I used on our trek. We make no claims to how it will work for you, only that it worked for us. Download the high-res lists at *www.doofus-dad.com/extras*. You can get to the Amazon product pages for most of it from the Hobnail Trekking gear page at *www.hobnailtrekking-co.com/gear*.

MARK'S GEAR LIST

BASE LAYERS

* Five (5) pairs of trekking socks (Swift-wick, Smartwool, and Darn Tough)
* Five (5) pairs of Merino wool boxer briefs (Apex and Ridge)
* Three (3) Merino wool t-shirts (WoolX) *I wish I'd brought two more.*
* One (1) pair of 260-count heavy Merino wool long underwear bottoms (MeriWool) *Only needed these one day.*
* One (1) pairs of 150-count mid-weight Merino wool long underwear bottoms (Smartwool)
* Two (2) 150-count Merino wool long underwear shirts (Icebreaker)
* One (1) 260-count Merino wool long underwear shirt (Icebreaker)

MID-LAYERS

* One (1) 250-count Merino wool long-sleeve mid-zip shirt (Sherpa Adventure Gear)
* One (1) long-sleeve, full zip, fleece jacket (Sherpa Adventure Gear)

OUTER LAYERS

* Three (3) pairs of convertible hiking pants (REI Screeline) *Wore these most of the time.*
* One (1) pair fleece-lined, wind-resistant hiking pants (Nonwe)
* One (1) 800-count hooded, down jacket (Montbell)

OTHER PERSONAL STUFF

* One (1) pair of convertible gloves (Outdoor Research Meteor Mitts). Most of the time, I used them without the outer shell.
* Fleece pajama bottoms and fleece top for tea house
* Lightweight sneakers for tea house
* Neck wallet (Lewis N. Clark)
* Two (2) beanies
* Polarized sunglasses, with a cheaper back-up pair
* 0-20° sleeping bag
* 35-liter backpack (Gregory Stout) with 3-liter Camelbak Hydration unit
* One (1) Steripen Ultra
* Asolo TPS 520 GV hiking boots
* One (1) Hobnail Trekking cap
* One (1) headlamp
* GoPro Hero 5 camera, backpack strap clamp, camera case, 5 GoPro batteries

* Zhiyun Smooth Q Camera Gimbal
* iPad with keyboard case
* ZeroLemon 26800 mAh SolarJuice power bank
* One (1) Nalgene bottle
* One (1) Camp towel
* One (1) Dry sack for backpack storage
* Two (2) pairs of compression socks for international flights
* Luggage locks
* Black Diamond Trail Pro Shock trekking poles
* Ear plugs
* Balaclava
* Pillow case
* Diamox, Ibuprofen, Tylenol, Pepto Bismol, Immodium, etc.
* Stuff sacks and plastic air-tight bags

HOLLY'S GEAR LIST

BASE LAYERS

* Three (3) pairs sock liners (Smartwool)
* Six (6) pairs hiking socks (Swiftwick)
* Two (2) Merino wool t-shirts (WoolX)
* One (1) 150-count Merion wool long-sleeve half-zip hoodie (Patagonia)
* Six pairs of Merino wool boy short underwear (Ridge and Stoic)
* One (1) pair of 260-count Merino wool long underwear bottoms (WoolX)
* Two (2) pairs of 150-count Merino wool long underwear bottoms (Ibex – didn't wear these)
* One (1) 260-count Merino wool long underwear shirt (WoolX)
* One (1) Hobnail long-sleeve most comfortable shirt in the world! ☺
* Two (2) Merino wool racerback sports bras (Smartwool, Ibex)
* One (1) 260-count Merino wool quarter zip (Icebreaker)
* One (1) long-sleeve synthetic t-shirt (Champion)
* Two (2) long-sleeve Merino wool t-shirt (WoolX)

MID-LAYERS

* One (1) Merino wool long-sleeved jacket with thumb holes (Outdoor Research)
* One (1) long-sleeve, full zip, fleece jacket (Columbia)

OUTER LAYERS

* One (1) pair hiking pants (Columbia)
* One (1) pair hiking tights (The North Face)
* One (1) pair fleece-lined hybrid tights (Outdoor Research)
* One (1) 800-count hooded down jacket (Arc'teryx)
* One (1) windbreaker rain jacket (Patagonia)

OTHER PERSONAL STUFF

* One (1) wool beanie (Sherpa Adventure Gear)
* One (1) Hobnail ball cap
* One (1) Nalgene bottle
* Baby lotion
* Foot care products (moleskin, rubber toe hugs)
* Headlamp (Black Diamond)
* Adult baby wipes (Klenz was awesome – towel sized!)
* Hand and Toe Warmers
* Extra shoe laces
* Tums
* Hiking boot (Oboz)
* 0-20° sleeping bag
* 25-liter daypack (Camelbak) with 3-liter bladder
* Lifestraw Go Filter Bottle w/2-stage filtration
* Hiking poles (Black Diamond)
* Four (4) buffs
* Neck wallet (Lewis N. Clark)
* Earplugs
* Luggage locks
* Stuff sacks and plastic bags
* Two (2) pairs UV sunglasses
* Lip balm
* Sunscreen
* Crossword puzzles
* Pee bottle
* Lightweight tea house sneakers
* Go Girl (she-nis)
* Kindle Fire
* Clean, dry clothes to put on once back in Kathmandu
* Eye mask and neck pillow for international flights
* Ear buds and charger for iPhone
* Diamox, Dramamine, Ibuprofen, Tylenol, Pepto Bismol, Immodium, etc.
* Airborne for the international flights
* Fleece pajamas to wear in teahouse
* Universal travel adapter
* One (1) balaclava
* One (1) pair glove liners (Swiftwick – wore these most of the time)
* One (1) pair gloves (Outdoor Research)
* Wide-brim hat
* Heavy gloves

APPENDIX C — TRAINING

There could be an entire book written just about training for this kind of trek. And even if there was, half of the world's population would probably disagree with most of the training recommendations.

So, I'll tell you what WE did.

Even though Holly and I had formerly been avid Crossfitters for five straight years, injuries had derailed our fitness routines for quite a while when we met Dawa in August 2016. So when we began training for Everest, we started with walking around our neighborhood and a running track at a nearby park.

Gotta start somewhere.

That quickly ramped up to hiking, and just as quickly, Holly was knocked out of commission due to surgeries.

While she recovered, I hiked. A lot. By the time we left for Nepal, I was hiking at least six miles a pop, three days a week. Usually, I was doing an eleven-mile circuit with a weighted backpack. My routes were almost always at state parks near our home in Middle Tennessee. Over time, I continued to increase my speed, tracking my progress on a fitness app. I knew the trails so well, I was on a first-name basis with the squirrels.

Because Holly couldn't do high-impact, we purchased a recumbent exercise bike, which she rode an hour a day almost daily for a couple months. I rode it on days between hiking.

The following guide gives you a good, basic guide. I recommend that you discuss this with your doc or trainer and tweak it as necessary.

NEPAL TREKKING TRAINING GUIDE

Hiking

Nothing is better for training for a trek than trekking! If you're starting from scratch, begin by walking 1/2 mile or mile each day. Progress to the point at which you can walk two or three miles at a brisk pace. Then, switch over to hiking boots and local trails. Start on relatively easy ground and work yourself up to more challenging routes. Consistentcy is key! Every day, try to push yourself a little farther and longer. By the time you depart for Nepal, you should be able to hike 5-7 hours straight for at least two consecutive days. You should also be wearing the daypack you'll have in Nepal with plenty of water and extra weight.

A word about running/jogging. This is clearly a great cardio exercise, but it's also high-impact and can be tough on knees. Running over pavement also works a different set of muscles than trail hiking, so if you want to run, we recommend you do it on a trail!

Body weight exercises

Hiking is great, but you should also add other type of workouts to stimulate your muscles. On days that you're not on the trail, do several sets of 10 or 20 consecutive:
- air squats
- walking lunges
- calf raises

When these begin feeling "easy," do them while wearing your weighted daypack.

Also add some upper-body/abdominal/combo movements like:
- pushups (against wall, on knees, or traditional)
- planks
- bear-crawls
- mountain-climbers
- chair dips

These will condition you for carrying your pack and improve your overall fitness.

Machines

If you have access to them, great machines to use are
- recumbent bicycle
- stairmaster
- eliptical

ABOUT HOBNAIL TREKKING CO.

We launched Hobnail Trekking after noticing that there were very few similar companies east of Colorado.

Why should the Western U.S. have all the fun, right?

Our goal was to create a company that Americans would feel comfortable dealing with, so that's how we've set it up. We also do a live event — the Everest Base Camp Trek Experience — at various venues around the Southeast U.S., so keep an eye out for us.

At the time of this writing, we are booking treks to Nepal only. We go to:

- Everest Base Camp
- Gokyo Lakes
- A combination of Gokyo Lakes + Everest Base Camp
- Annapurna Base Camp
- The Annapurna Circuit, and
- Poon Hill.

To learn all about Hobnail Trekking, visit us online at *www.hobnailtrekkingco.com*. I will be embarking on at least one trek myself per year (for the foreseeable future), and it would be wicked cool if you came along.

ACKNOWLEDGMENTS

You may be tempted to believe that this entire book is the product of my own fevered, doofus mind, but that wouldn't be entirely accurate.

First of all, it would've been impossible without the unwavering support — in all ways possible — of my wife, Holly. Not only did she play a pivotal role in the story itself, she also encouraged (forced) me to write it down, clearing my schedule (wasn't difficult), and keeping the kids and cats away from the office (not really) while I worked. She also kindly pointed out everything that was wrong with the first draft, made me fix it, and then sighed and fixed it herself.

Even though our kids haven't really noticed anything that has happened with their parents over the past two years, including the fact that we were gone for three weeks, I thank them — Sam, Ava, and Pete — for being the World's Best Chi-ren and not burning down the house. They inspire me every day.

Huge thanks go to my dear friend, Dawa. The adventure would not have happened without him. It's as simple as that.

To our wonderful friend and neighbor, Kathy Helmers, I bow in deference. A talented editor, writer, and literary agent, she helped make this book legible and has been an invaluable source of information.

Thanks so much to Doug Holmquist, who recorded and produced the audiobook and read Alan Arnette's foreword. What a fun, crazy process.

To my old compadre, Dennis Ritchie, enormous gratitude for the many years of tireless encouragement and creative brain-storming.

Big thanks to our neighborhood "Village" members: Mike and Dayna Tharpe, Eric and Shanna Helm, Justin and Nikki Gersman, Justin and Andrea Miers, Scott Saul, and John and Beverly Boyle.

Eternal thanks, of course, go to the trekkers you met in this book. Talk about a leap of faith!

Thanks also to mountaineering legend Alan Arnette, who agreed to write a foreword for this book for some newbie he hardly knows.

Lastly, I bestow all possible gratitude on my parents, Hal and Sarah Johnson, for making me understand all those years ago that I could do anything — even trekking to Mt. Everest and writing a book about it — if I only believed in myself. Look, Ma! Look, Pa!

ONE LAST THING FOR YOU, DEAR READER

Thank you TONS for reading this book. After all those years as a writer, this is my very first book, so you spending the time to read it means a lot.

If you liked it, you could impress your friends and family by writing me a review on the Amazon product page and letting them know about it.

(Unless you hated it. Then don't write a review and don't tell anyone.)

And as I've mentioned before, get access to videos, photos, gear lists, and various other free downloads at my "Extras" page by visiting *www.doofusdad.com/extras.*

Thanks again!

ABOUT THE AUTHOR

Mark E. Johnson has been a writer in some capacity since he began penning poetry as a six-year-old. Over the ensuing years, he has worked as a road musician and Nashville songwriter; a journalist/editor in the fields of agriculture, rural living, and wildlife conservation; a freelance writer for various magazines; and a humorist/blogger. Given this white-bread, run-of-the-mill career trajectory, it was only natural that he would launch a Nepal trekking company in 2017 from his home base of Middle Tennessee.

Mark lives in Kingston Springs, Tennessee, with his wife, Holly, their three kids — Sam, Ava, and Pete — and two cats, CeCe and Greta.

Photo of the author on facing page by Bill Shupp.

GET THE AUDIOBOOK!

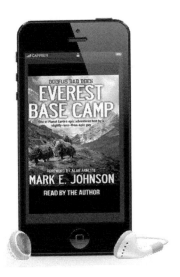

Simply visit *https://www.doofusdad.com/ebc-audiobook/*, follow the instructions, and download the audiobook immediately. Hope you enjoy it!

ALSO BY MARK E. JOHNSON

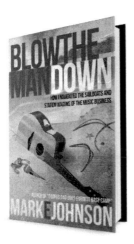

Blow the Man Down: How I navigated the sailboats and station wagons of the music business

In the 1970s, Mark Johnson was a gangly North Carolina farm boy with a big imagination. An avid reader of Doc Savage pulp novels and Hardy Boys Mysteries, Johnson knew he wanted adventure in his life. He just had no idea where to get it or how to escape the Christmas tree fields of the Appalachians. As an even ganglier teenager, Johnson discovered music. Then, girls. These epiphanies would lead to an adventure even Johnson's wild imagination couldn't have predicted.

In this "Doofus Dad" prequel, follow along as Johnson navigates a heart-pounding and often hilarious odyssey through the 1980s and '90s music industry as a songwriter and club musician, both in fickle Nashville and the mysterious Caribbean island of ill repute, St. Croix. Johnson reveals both the seductions and the hard truths of life in the world of entertainment.

Manufactured by Amazon.ca
Bolton, ON